Faith Flow

A Poetic Devotional for the Creative Soul

Jesus said to him, "If you can believe, all things *are* possible to him who believes."
–Mark 9:23 NKJV

"I can do all things through Christ who strengthens me."
–Philippians 4:13 NKJV

FAITH FLOW

A POETIC DEVOTIONAL FOR
THE CREATIVE SOUL

DEMETERIUS "FLITE" SMITH

DECREE™
PUBLISHING

FAITH FLOW

For speaking engagements, contact info is as follows:

Demeterius Smith

PO Box 8862, Greenville, SC 29604

- or - FLITE@lifedecreed.com / 864-735-3133

Subscribe to the blog: WWW.FLITESFAITHFLOW.WORDPRESS.COM

Manufactured in the United States of America

"THOU SHALT NOT STEAL." -Exodus 20:15, KJV

DECREE™
PUBLISHING

For my wife, my love and my best bud

Deneshia Graham Smith

Through you, God has made my life so much better.

Poetry   **Other Contents**

Poetry Other Contents

INTRODUCTION

Have you ever felt stuck in life? Is fear secretly holding you back from achieving your dreams? Could you use some fresh motivation?

If you answered "yes," then *Faith Flow* is for you. *Faith Flow* will ignite your passion, challenge you to challenge fear and give you practical steps to apply faith to every area of your life.

This book is written as a real life example of applying the principles contained within its pages. It is also written with your schedule in mind. *Faith Flow* can be read all at once if you desire, but it is designed for you to read one chapter each week over the course of a year.

Faith Flow can be used for individual edification, book clubs, small groups, cell groups, sermon illustrations and more. This isn't just a book; *Faith Flow* is creative ministry in action.

Faith Flow is divided into 52 chapters (weeks). Each week contains a devotional called a Flow. The Flows have four sections: a poem, Living Water, Poetic Insight, and Walk Out The Word. Each poem inspires and teaches a lesson from God's word. Living Water contains scripture references that support what is taught in the poem. Poetic Insight offers a look into the motivation behind the poem and highlights how the poem applies to our everyday lives. In Walk Out The Word the reader receives instruction on how to practically apply the lesson to their life.

Excerpt from Week 18:

_____

WOMEN OF PURPOSE

God never makes mistakes
He makes masterpieces
Water was never intended to be dry
Grass was never intended to be blue
And I guarantee every woman,
That God knew
Exactly what He was doing when He made you…

LIVING WATER:

"Many daughters have done well,
But you excel them all."
Charm is deceitful and beauty is passing,
But a woman who fears the LORD, she shall be praised."

Proverbs 31: 29-30 NKJV™

POETIC INSIGHT:

Women are sometimes undervalued by society. Everyday there are women who are abused by their husbands and/or disrespected by their children. Some women are made to feel poorly about themselves if they don't have a husband or child. Many women are still paid less money for doing the same level work as a man and dehumanized as sexual objects.

However, regardless of what society says, you are who God says you are. Every single woman is handcrafted by God. Stop calling yourself ugly, fat, or stupid. Stop thinking that you are not smart enough or pretty enough. You don't have to give up your integrity or purity. Stop thinking the abuse was your fault. No, you did not deserve to be cheated on. Don't be afraid to go after your dreams. God knows exactly who you are and he loves you as you are.

This is just an example of the many topics contained within this book. There is something for man and woman, teen and adult, even believer and non-believer. Some topics are light hearted, but some are challenging. Along with faith, hope, purpose and love, topics such as domestic violence, sexual purity, and absentee fathers are addressed. Prepare to be encouraged, prepare to be challenged, and prepare to be changed. I invite you to experience Faith Flow, feed your soul, and let your creative waters flow.

GO, BE GREAT

Don't give up, you weren't built for that
Don't settle, you're better than that
Don't shrink back, now isn't the time for that
Don't cave in, you're greater than that

You are eternity
Wrapped in time
Look internally
So your eternal can shine

You are more than you have become
Your calling is higher than what you do
You are expected to achieve greatness
Because great is the God in you

No more just getting by
No more depression clouds
No more half-hearted tries
Wasting minutes is not allowed

Be as steadfast as the mountain
Yet as agile as the river
God has filled you with greatness
And He expects you to deliver

Go forth and conquer
Make haste, you are late
Display your God-given greatness,
For the world eagerly awaits

Living Water:

"For I consider that the sufferings of this present time are not worthy to be compared with the glory which shall be revealed in us. For the earnest expectation of the creation eagerly waits for the revealing of the sons of God. For the creation was subjected to futility, not willingly, but because of Him who subjected it in hope;" -Romans 8:18-20 NKJV™

"Most assuredly, I say to you, he who believes in Me, the works that I do he will do also; and greater works than these he will do, because I go to My Father. And whatever you ask in My name, that I will do, that the Father may be glorified in the Son." -John 14:11-13 NKJV™

Poetic Insight:

Do you flirt with the idea of throwing in the towel? Do you feel as if you're settling for mediocrity? If you could answer "yes" to either question, stop living beneath what you can achieve. God has given each of us a purpose to fulfill on the earth. Your purpose is your challenge to meet. It doesn't matter how educated you are, who your parents were or were not or the obstacles you've already faced. What matters is that you return to the Father with a return on what He's given you to work with.

Somewhere, there is a problem and in fulfilling your purpose, you hold the answer.

Walk Out The Word:

Ask God to help you to understand your purpose in life. You may not receive your answer immediately, but trust that he is answering you in a way that will be relevant to you. Your purpose will be made clear. As you wait, continue to study the word of God and seek out some resources that can help guide you as you seek to understand your purpose. May I suggest the book, "The Purpose Driven Life" by Rick Warren.

LIPS OF LIFE

Like the painter's brush bringing forth beauty
On a canvas that is empty
The words that come from my mouth
Will color every moment of life that is yet to be

If I speak expectations haunted
By past pains, failures and fears
Then the same ol' mess from my yesterdays
Will stink up my New Year

You see?
Like the grass is left wet by the morning dew
On my lips
What I love will leave its residue

My tongue powers life or death
No one else's choice, I choose
If I choose wrong, it becomes my burden
And ultimately, I lose

So I decide to speak with care
Since my words push good or bad into the atmosphere
I speak what God has spoken over me
Destroying words uttered to the contrary

My lips are lips of life
Scripture-filled declarations go before me
And a life of faith, abundance, joy
Will be manifested to me and my family

Living Water:

"Death and life are in the power of the tongue, And those who love it will eat its fruit." -Proverbs 18:21 NKJV™

Poetic Insight:

As a child you may have heard or recited the following saying: "Sticks and stones may break my bones, but words will never hurt me." That saying is not true. Words can hurt and words can destroy. Every day, people use words to discourage, deflate dreams, imprison hope and confuse sound minds. Words can be a weapon used against you.

We often fail to realize that words are not passive, they are powerful. Words can free you. Words can empower and embolden you. Words can bring you clarity of mind and inspiration for your life. Words can help you heal.

Perhaps you've heard Christian believers talk about "speaking life." It's become a bit of a catch phrase and a principle that has gained attention in recent years. But speaking life is not a trend that will pass. It's wisdom, extracted from God's word that tells us that our words should be used with wisdom and precision. Each day, train your lips to be lips of life.

WALK OUT THE WORD:

Utilize the following exercise as you begin to transform that way you speak about your life: Take a sheet of notebook paper and draw a vertical line down the middle. At the top of the page on the left side, write the word CAN'T. Write the word CAN at the top of the page on the right side.

Under the word CAN'T write down 5-10 things that have been said (by you or others) that have been hurtful or negative. This can include what you can't do, can't achieve, can't have, etc. Be honest with yourself; you don't have to share your list with anyone. Under the word CAN write down the following scripture, "I CAN DO ALL THINGS THROUGH CHRIST WHO STRENGTHENS ME," PHILIPPIANS 4:13 NKJV.

Counter every negative comment you've written by speaking aloud this scripture. You don't need to give voice to the negative; give voice only to the truth. As you do this daily, you should begin to feel more strength and more courage to overcome the words and mindsets that have held you back.

I BELIEVE

I believe God created the heavens and the earth
I believe God formed man from the dust
I believe God blew his breath into humanity
Extending to us purpose, dominion and worth

I BELIEVE

I believe Jesus is God's spotless son
I believe God so loved the world
That He gave His only begotten one
A holy seed sown for a harvest of daughters and sons

I BELIEVE

I believe with my heart and confess my sins
Jesus reconnected us to God for a world without end
The price paid, God raised his son to life again
And I am saved according to verse nine of Romans chapter ten, amen

I BELIEVE

LIVING WATER:

"That if you confess with your mouth the Lord Jesus and believe in your heart that God has raised Him from the dead, you will be saved."
- Romans 10:9 NKJV™

POETIC INSIGHT:

Every so often we should remind ourselves of what we believe and why we believe it. In terms of our Christian walk, this reminder is neither a reassessment nor a review of the necessity of our faith. Instead, this reminder is a reaffirmation of our faith, and a renewal of our commitment to follow Christ's lordship.

Perhaps you are reading this and you have not received Christ's salvation. When Jesus died on the cross for our sins, he made salvation available to anyone who would receive him and believe in him. You can have salvation this day by believing the words of this prayer and reciting it aloud:

"Lord Jesus, I am a sinner and I stand in need. I come to you in prayer to ask for the salvation that you made available through your death on the cross. I believe God raised you from the dead and I confess that you are Lord. Please come into my heart and lead me forward in your will. It's in your name I pray, amen."

If you prayed this prayer, according to Romans 10:9, you are saved! Congratulations! Purchase a Holy Bible; consider a version (wording) of the Bible that you can easily understand. Then, begin attending a Bible-believing church, which will help you grow in your faith.

WALK OUT THE WORD:

This day, remind yourself of what you believe as a follower of Jesus Christ. Then, write down what you believe and post it where you will look at it daily (bathroom mirror, refrigerator door, planner, school notebook, etc.)

ALL THINGS ARE POSSIBLE

With God:

All things are possible
Nothing is impossible

Possible... All things
Impossible... No thing

God, You are almighty
All mighty are You
God, You are awesome
Father, Your every word is true

God, You are omniscient
Father, You are omnipresent
God, You are omnipotent
On You, there are no limits

God, You are with me
And I am with You
Be who you promised to be to me
Do what you promised to do
For with you

All things are possible
Nothing is impossible

Possible... All things
Impossible... No thing

LIVING WATER:

"But Jesus looked at them and said to them, "With men this is impossible, but with God all things are possible." -Matthew 19:26 NKJV™

"Jesus said to him, "If you can believe, all things are possible to him who believes." -Mark 9:23 NKJV™

God is not limited by my experiences, my past, my failures, my successes, my present, my knowledge, my comprehension, my imagination, my gifts, my family, my connections, my friends, my talents or my ability to understand. He is not limited by what I have seen, what I have read or what has happened in someone else's life.

God is not limited. Nonetheless, the Christian believer can limit the move of God in his or her life due to a lack of faith. Have you employed faith lately? I'm not talking about faith for some material thing that can be purchased. I'm talking about the faith that firmly believes in God's sovereignty and knows He is able to make impossible things happen.

WALK OUT THE WORD:

Get three sheets of paper. On the first sheet write "Characteristics of God". Under that, write down a word describing something about God's character such as faithful, holy or loving.

Next, find a scripture that talks about that characteristic and write down the scripture. Under the scripture write down a paragraph telling about how God has shown himself to you in that way. By doing this you will gain a clearer understanding of God's personality.

Please see the examples I provide on the following page.

Example:

> ## Characteristics of God
>
> FORGIVING
>
> "If we confess our sins, he is faithful and just to forgive us our sins, and to cleanse us from all unrighteousness."
>
> -1 John 1:9
>
> *God has promised to forgive me for things I've done wrong. He is faithful, so I can trust that what he tells me in His word is true.*

On the second sheet write down "I am believing God for:" at the top of the paper. Then write down three things that you want God to do in your life.

Example:

> ## "I am believing God for:"
>
> 1.) The grace to win souls to Christ on my job.
>
> 2.) The resources needed for me to get my college education.
>
> 3.) The willpower to quit smoking.

On the third sheet write down "Power Professions". Professions are statements you will speak aloud that support what you're believing for. Write your own professions about your life based off what you have studied about God's characteristics and based off what you are believing God to do in your life. Then, begin speaking your professions.

Example:

> ## "Power Professions"
>
> Today, I profess that with God all things are possible. God is loving and forgiving. God will give me the willpower to quit smoking. God will use this demonstration of His power in my life to win others to Christ. God will provide me with the resources I need to get my college education. I will be a college graduate. I speak and expect these things in Jesus name. Amen.

On all three sheets make what you write down relevant and meaningful to you. Don't worry about whether you're doing it correctly. As you grow in your faith, God will increase your understanding. If you make a mistake, He has the grace and compassion to cover you.

Continue to speak daily what you have written down. And, be mindful that your behavior begins to line up with what you are professing. For example, if someone made the profession to quit smoking, then that person shouldn't sit in the smoking section of a restaurant. A person professing for resources to go to college should start looking for scholarships. Begin to live according to what you want to see manifested in your life.

Finally, be patient. Don't give up. Allow room for God's timing and allow yourself a measure of grace for the mistakes and missteps you will surely make. This is a process of change. Some changes will be harder to make than others. Most will not happen instantly. But, keep speaking truth about yourself and your life, rely on God's faithfulness and get ready to enjoy the fruit of your lips and the reward of your faith.

FREE

I am F-R-E-E
Faithfully Reigning over Every Enemy
There are no chains holding me
I am FREE

FREE from the lies
FREE from my mistakes
FREE from the rage that came from heartaches

I am F-R-E-E
Faithfully Reigning over Every Enemy
I can do all things through Christ who strengthens me
I am FREE

FREE to give God glory
FREE to fulfill my destiny
FREE to laugh and have peace and joy within me
FREE to impact earth for eternity

With God all things are possible
I am Faithfully Reigning over Every Enemy
No chains hold me
Glory to God, I am FREE!

LIVING WATER:

"Therefore if the Son makes you free, you shall be free indeed."
-John 8:36 NKJV™

"Behold, I give you the authority to trample on serpents and scorpions, and over all the power of the enemy, and nothing shall by any means hurt you. Nevertheless do not rejoice in this, that the spirits are subject to you, but rather rejoice because your names are written in heaven." -Luke 10:19-20 NKJV™

POETIC INSIGHT:

To watch a child at play is to witness a life of fearlessness and possibilities. While the child is in his or her own world of imagination, nearby, there is usually a watchful adult who is careful to remove any harmful or dangerous thing from the child's reach.

When Jesus made us free through salvation, he told us our punishment – separation from God – was over and we could come out to play. We were free to live an abundant life and enjoy beneficial things while he carefully watched over us and directed our paths.

Are you playing? Are you exploring the known gifts God placed inside of you and asking him to reveal the hidden talents you possess? It's time to be free.

Freedom allows you to Faithfully Reign over Every Enemy. The word "faithfully" is key. You must remain faithful to God and his ways to fully realize the freedom that is yours. And once you've stepped into this world of fearlessness and possibilities, you reign in victory over any enemy.

WALK OUT THE WORD:

Sometimes, you must overcome yourself to gain freedom. Repeating past mistakes and failures in your mind and heart will keep you imprisoned and afraid to move forward.

What have you always wanted to do, but were afraid to attempt for fear of failure or rejection. Today, do one thing that will get you a step closer to realizing that dream. Each day continue to take a step in the direction of that dream.

HEALING

As the cat-of-nine-tails ripped His skin
From the moment it went in, to Jesus' back
Before the soldier could pull his hand back
Tearing the precious flesh piece by piece
My total and complete healing was released

As He hung on the cross, all hope seemingly lost
Bearing my grief and carrying my sorrows –
For my sins He paid full cost
Smitten by God
The chastisement for my peace was upon the king
Royalty was bruised for my iniquities
And now His praises I sing

The Son of Righteousness shall arise
With healing in His wings
For I fear the name Jehovah-Rapha
And there is not one thing
He did not ordain to be
That can take up residence inside of me

Right now I speak
To every sickness, disease, germ, virus,
Health crisis, abnormal condition, plague and/or calamity
Let it be known that by royal decree
You are out of order and trespassing
If you attempt to come on or into me
Because I am God's property
Jesus finished His work at Calvary
And now holds the deed to my body
Therefore, I declare in the name of Jesus Christ
That any and every sickness, disease, germ, virus,
Health crisis, abnormal condition, plaque and/or calamity
That touches and/or appears in my body

Dies and is completely removed instantly
Without causing any hurt, harm or danger to me
For you see
Every cell, organ, tissue, bone, vein, artery
Every aspect of my being and every part of my body
Functions absolutely perfectly
For that is exactly
How God created and ordained it to be

I am H-E-A-L-E-D
I am healed
And that's sealed
For all eternity
I am healed physically, spiritually, financially,
Socially, emotionally and mentally
This declaration and acceptance
Of my total and complete healing isn't just for me
It also covers my family currently
And extends into the future
Covering my family that is to be

That's right...my entire bloodline
I got blood work done
The results came back
Saying that I had the blood of the Son
God's only Begotten One
The King of Kings, Lord of Lords
The Good Shepherd, the manifested Living Sword
With whom I am a joint heir
For you see
The x-rays reveal that there is a king inside of me
So I walk in the full authority
Of the priest and the K-I-N-G
Enjoying full liberty
Because my High Priest and King
Has set me free
And this is the way it has to be

Because the word of God states
For all the Kingdom and world to see
In 1 Peter 5:10 that by Christ Jesus
The God of all grace has called me
To His eternal glory!

LIVING WATER:

"Who has believed our report? And to whom has the arm of the LORD been revealed? For He shall grow up before Him as a tender plant, And as a root out of dry ground. He has no form or comeliness; And when we see Him, There is no beauty that we should desire Him. He is despised and rejected by men, A Man of sorrows and acquainted with grief. And we hid, as it were, our faces from Him; He was despised, and we did not esteem Him. Surely He has borne our grief And carried our sorrows; Yet we esteemed Him stricken, Smitten by God, and afflicted. But He was wounded for our transgressions, He was bruised for our iniquities; The chastisement for our peace was upon Him, And by His stripes we are healed." -Isaiah 53:1-5 NKJV™

POETIC INSIGHT:

This poem is meant to be read aloud as a declaration of our healing in Christ Jesus. God is a healer and He can free you from the chains of any sickness you face. We cannot hurry a move of God, and we may not understand why he allows some things to occur. But, we can boldly declare the truth of His word; which clearly outlines a plan for our healing long before our birth. Some people are healed in an instant after an encounter with God, some people are healed over time because they go to the doctor and take their medicine, and some people are healed once they depart from this life.

This poem is a declaration of life and healing that you should speak out loud.

Not only do I challenge you to speak life, I also challenge you to begin to change your lifestyle.

We are always busy, always on the go, always going to work, always going to help...We are always moving, but are we getting anywhere?

There are seasons when more will be required of you, but remember these two things:

1.) ALWAYS is not a season

2.) You can't help anyone if you allow yourself to be neglected

God made the heavens and the earth, and then **God RESTED**. (Genesis 2:3)

Jesus often got away from the crowd and His disciples to spend time alone with God the Father. (Matthew 14:23)
Knowledge that isn't used is wasted, and faith without works is dead. You can know that you need to change the oil in your car and you can speak in faith that "Oil you will be changed." But, if you never go to the mechanic, that car is going to put you down. You will destroy the engine and shorten the "life span" of the vehicle. Why is it that we make sure to take care of something that can be replaced (like a car) but we take a half-hearted approach to consistently care for that which cannot be replaced (ourselves)?

WALK OUT THE WORD:

Recite *HEALING* daily for the coming week and read Isaiah 53:1-5 twice a day. Begin to solidify the truth of God's word in your heart. Ask God for wisdom in your area of need (physical healing, financial healing, spiritual healing, etc.) Be on the lookout for God's answers in usual and unusual ways. Then, simply do as He instructs.

F.I.S.H.

Finally, It Shall Happen
Everything I've been praying about
Everything I've been shouting about
Everything I've been dreaming about

After all the naysayers
After all the prayer haters
After all the fuss and stress
After all the mess –
Yet, still I am blessed

It couldn't hold me
It couldn't stop me
Not the woman running interference
Nor the man trying to block me

Finally, It Shall Happen
God's word cannot be denied
My expectation has me salivating
Like I'm standing in line anticipating
A plate with coleslaw and hush puppies on the side
At the Friday night fish fry

LIVING WATER:

"And when Jesus went out He saw a great multitude; and He was moved with compassion for them, and healed their sick. When it was evening, His disciples came to Him, saying, "This is a deserted place, and the hour is already late. Send the multitudes away, that they may go into the villages and buy themselves food." But Jesus said to them, "They do not need to go away. You give them something to eat." And they said to Him, "We have here only five loaves and two fish." He said, "Bring them here to Me." Then He commanded the multitudes to sit down on the grass. And He took the five loaves and the two fish, and looking up to heaven, He blessed and broke and gave the loaves to the disciples; and the disciples gave to the multitudes. So they all ate and were filled, and they took up twelve baskets full of the fragments that remained. Now those who had eaten were about five thousand men, besides women and children." - Matthew 14:14-21 NKJV™

"When He had stopped speaking, He said to Simon, "Launch out into the deep and let down your nets for a catch." But Simon answered and said to Him, "Master, we have toiled all night and caught nothing; nevertheless at Your word I will let down the net." And when they had done this, they caught a great number of fish, and their net was breaking. So they signaled to their partners in the other boat to come and help them. And they came and filled both the boats, so that they began to sink." - Luke 5:4-7 NKJV™

POETIC INSIGHT:

Finally It Shall Happen! The things that God promised you shall happen. It doesn't matter how impossible it may seem. Your resources may not be great, but take what you have and with faith put it in God's hands. When the little boy handed over his two pieces of fish and five loaves of bread Jesus used it to feed over five thousand people.

You may have already given up on the hopes and dreams you had. It is time for you to go back out there and go after your promise. It doesn't matter if you have already given it your best shot and failed miserably, go back out there and dig deep again. Simon (who is called Peter) said to Jesus we toiled all night and caught nothing, NEVERTHELESS at Your word I will let down my net.

You may have already tried...Nevertheless

Someone may have lied...Nevertheless

 A loved one died...Nevertheless

A friend walked away...Nevertheless

Got bills you cannot pay...Nevertheless

You failed the last time...Nevertheless

You sinned and don't feel blessed...Nevertheless

What God has promised is guaranteed. Finally It Shall Happen for you!

WALK OUT THE WORD:

Encourage yourself; remember God's faithfulness throughout your life. What has he already brought you through or out of? Think about those times when you sought God for something urgent and think about his responses to you. Remember the goodness of the Lord. Then, begin to awaken those promises with what you speak.

WHO ARE YOU?

I am Chosen
Called, selected, favored

I am Loved
Cherished, treasured, cared for

I am Forgiven
Exonerated, acquitted, pardoned

I am the Head
Champion, captain, chief

I am Blessed
Endowed, empowered, anointed

I am Beautiful
Magnificent, timely, flourishing

I am God's
Saved, redeemed, accepted

I am who I AM says I am
Who are you?

LIVING WATER:

"And He said, Your name shall be called no more Jacob [supplanter], but Israel [contender with God]; for you have contended and have power with God and with men and have prevailed. Then Jacob asked Him, Tell me, I pray You, what [in contrast] is Your name? But He said, Why is it that you ask My name? And [the Angel of God declared] a blessing on [Jacob] there." -Genesis 32:28-29 AMP

POETIC INSIGHT:

Jacob's name was changed to Israel after he encountered God in the 32nd chapter of Genesis. Jacob's actions defined who he was and the definition wasn't good: Trickster.

His encounter with God placed a blessing on him; Jacob needed a new way to define himself based on who God said he was.

When we receive Christ's offer of salvation, we are made new. We don't have to change our legal name, but we should disassociate ourselves with past mistakes and bad actions. Redefine who you are, according to God's standards.

WALK OUT THE WORD:

Go on a negativity fast. For seven days, refuse to speak or think anything negative about yourself or others. Counter any negative thoughts with a word of truth about your identity and how God defines his people.

I AM BEAUTIFUL

I am made in the image of God
I am beautiful

I was knitted together in my mother's womb
I am beautiful

I am purposed by God
I am beautiful

God loves me
I am beautiful

You are made in the image of God
You are beautiful

You were knitted together in your mother's womb
You are beautiful

God has a purpose for your life
You are beautiful

God loves you
You are a beautiful creation of God

Yes, you are beautiful

LIVING WATER:

"For you created my inmost being; you knit me together in my mother's womb. I praise you because I am fearfully and wonderfully made; your works are wonderful, I know that full well. My frame was not hidden from you when I was made in the secret place. When I was woven together in the depths of the earth, your eyes saw my unformed body. All the days ordained for me were written in your book before one of them came to be. How precious to me are your thoughts, O God! How vast is the sum of them!" -Psalm 139:13-17 NIV

"God said, Let Us [Father, Son, and Holy Spirit] make mankind in Our image, after Our likeness, and let them have complete authority over the fish of the sea, the birds of the air, the [tame] beasts, and over all of the earth, and over everything that creeps upon the earth. So God created

man in His own image, in the image and likeness of God He created him; male and female He created them." -Genesis 1:26-27 AMP

"For God so loved the world that he gave his only begotten Son, that whosoever believeth in him should not perish, but have everlasting life. For God sent not his Son into the world to condemn the world; but that the world through him might be saved." -John 3:16-17 KJV

POETIC INSIGHT:

"Have you ever stopped to think about just how amazing of a creation you are? It may sound like a cliché but it is sincere and true that, "God made you special." You are a designer original! Why, did He do that? Love was his motivation. No matter how ugly you may feel and no matter what ugly things you may have done, God designed you to be beautiful. Stop and look at yourself. Not just your outer appearances, but look at how precious life is and how magnificent of a creation you are.

I'm not telling you to be prideful and conceited. Instead I am inviting you to be humbled by the love of God. You are beautiful, not because of anything you have done, or haven't done, but because he loves you enough to have formed you. I can't tell you that life will be easier with him, but I can tell you that life will be better. You were not designed to live without his love. You are beautiful because you are made and loved by a beautiful God. (The one, true, and living God.) God loves you, God loves you, God loves you. Yes, God loves you!

WALK OUT THE WORD:

Focus your attention on the God we serve. What makes him beautiful to you? Write down seven attributes of God and praise him for each one each day of the coming week.

I AM NOT AFRAID

Once upon a time I was afraid
I felt scared to death
Running for my life
While trying to catch my breath

I could feel them getting closer
From the darkness, shadows lurked
I tried to out run them
Alas, it didn't work

"You can never run fast enough,"
Said a mysterious voice
"Turn and face them,"
"You have no choice"

Slowly I rotated
Tired, sweaty, aggravated
They laughed wickedly
Calmly, I waited

The shadows jumped
Click, I connected with all my might
The shadows fled
Click, I turned back off the light

LIVING WATER:

"Casting down imaginations, and every high thing that exalteth itself
against the knowledge of God, and bringing into captivity every thought to
the obedience of Christ;" 2 Corinthians 10:5 KJV

If the Son therefore shall make you free, ye shall be free indeed. -John
8:36 KJV

For God hath not given us the spirit of fear; but of power, and of love, and
of a sound mind. -2 Timothy 1:7 KJV

There is no fear in love; but perfect love casteth out fear: because fear
hath torment. He that feareth is not made perfect in love. -1 John 4:18 KJV

POETIC INSIGHT:

Fear is afraid of God.

WALK OUT THE WORD:

"If A = B, and B = C, then A = C. Your thoughts control what you speak (A). What you speak controls your life (B). Then, it's true that what you think will control your life (A=C).

If fear controls your thoughts, then fear will control your life (and imprison you in the process). Don't allow your mind and heart to imprison you. Renew your mind with God's word so that your thoughts will be control by the word of God. Then you will speak the word of God about you and your life. Then you and your life will be better, (not necessarily easier) then you ever imagined. You are not a victim, you are a vibrant victorious victor. You are no longer a hostage; you are now a hero. Take this truth and go rescue someone else from the prison of their mind. Embrace God's love and live the full, free, and fulfilling life God designed for you. FEAR NOT.......YOU ARE FREE!

LET THERE BE...

Let there be ...
No hidden sins within me
My heart regards no iniquity
I worship God only, in spirit and in truth

Let there be...
I obey God wholeheartedly
I follow His instructions completely, immediately
I love God with all my heart, soul, mind, strength
With God I share the closest intimacy

Let there be...

Let there be...
I love my neighbors just like I love me
I operate by God's grace for His glory
With genuine humility
Seeking the Kingdom of God
His righteousness is my top priority

Let there be...
All the things I need are added unto me
By Christ Jesus, God supplies all
My needs according to His riches in glory
My soul prospers abundantly

Let there be...

Let there be...
 I am strong and healthy
I can do all things through Christ
Who strengthens me
For the Spirit of the Lord dwells inside
His son, setting me free, indeed

Let there be...
Prayer constantly
Pleasing God continuously
No weapon formed shall prosper against me
I am more than a conqueror

Let there be...
For the Lord, I wait patiently, expectantly

I dwell in the secret place of the most High
And abide under the shadow of the Almighty

Let there be...
The angels of God keep me in all my ways
They keep charge over me
I delight myself in the Lord
The desires of my heart are given unto me

Let there be...
The Lord keeps me going in, coming out
I bless the Lord at all times
His praise continually in my mouth

Let there be...

Let there be...
 I am kept in perfect peace
In wisdom and stature I increase
Favor with God and man
In all my getting, I understand

Let there be...
 I meditate on the law of the Lord day and night
I walk by faith, not by sight
Enjoying an absence of lack in my life

Let there be...
I sow good seeds into good ground, bountifully
At least a hundredfold harvest is returned unto me
The Lord anoints me fresh, daily
I have the armor of God on me, security
Always followed by goodness and mercy

Let there be...
I live each day with joy and victory
Angels of God recognize my authority
They go forth to manifest the words of this decree
Immediately

Let there be...

LIVING WATER:

"Death and life are in the power of the tongue, and those who love it will eat its fruit." –Proverbs 18:21

Poetic Insight:

Regarding your life, you are an artist. Your life is the blank canvas. Your tongue is the paintbrush. The words you choose are the colors. With every stroke of your paintbrush (every time you speak) you affect the picture that will become your life. God spoke the whole world into existence. We are created in His image and given creative ability along with a certain amount of authority. We've also been told in Galatians 6:7b that what we sow we shall reap. Proverbs 18:21 tell us that death and life are in the power of the tongue: and they that love it shall eat the fruit thereof.

If you want the picture of your life to become a masterpiece then start painting with the Master's colors (God's word)!

Walk Out The Word:

Find out what God says about you. Believe what God says about you. Speak the things that God has said about you.

Now faith is the substance of things hoped for, the evidence of things not seen.

Hebrews 11:1 KJV

WEAPONS OF MASS DESTRUCTION

Can't
                    Never
                                    Weak
Stupid
                    Ugly
                                    Defeat
Loser
                    Idiot
                                    Impossible
Poor
                    No Way
                                    Miserable
Too Much
                    Negative
                                    Hopeless
Kill
                    Hate
                                    Worthless
Desperate
                    Depressed
                                    Downcast
Good for nothing
                    Sorry
                                    Wont' Last

LIVING WATER:

"Death and life are in the power of the tongue, and those who love it will eat its fruit." –Proverbs 18:21 NKJV™

Poetic Insight:

Words can be used as weapons. We can kill and destroy with what we say and the devastation can last a lifetime. Train yourself to use your weapon wisely. This includes when you speak about yourself and when you speak to and about others.

Walk Out The Word:

Words can also be used as weapons of mass *construction*. What you say can empower, encourage and eliminate doubt in the hearts of the hearers. This poem contains 24 phrases that are commonly used to berate others. This week, write down 12 words and/or phrases that edify others and begin using them. Here's one phrase to start: "You are important to me."

I WILL NOT

I will not blame my actions on someone else
For myself I take full responsibility
I will not scream, curse and "go crazy"
When someone is treating me unfairly

I will not explode on a person
For driving on the interstate slowly
I will not "fly off the handle"
If the waiter accidentally
Spills my sweet tea

I will not act ungodly
Even if others act ungodly toward me
What comes natural to some
Is no longer my reality

I will not hate my co-workers
Even when they are on my nerve, the very last
I will not undermine my boss
For acting like a complete @$%

I will not think thoughts
like the one I just had
Sure, saying it is different from thinking it
But thinking it is still bad

I will not "lay down my religion"
In order to lose control
My relationship with Jesus is too precious
To forfeit the fate of my soul

I will not allow the things I cannot control
To take control of me
I cannot stop certain things from happening
But I can choose to respond with positivity

LIVING WATER:

"Then He said to the disciples, "It is impossible that no offenses should come, but woe to him through whom they do come! It would be better for him if a millstone were hung around his neck, and he were thrown into the sea, than that he should offend one of these little ones. Take heed to yourselves. If your brother sins against you, rebuke him; and if he repents,

forgive him. And if he sins against you seven times in a day, and seven times in a day returns to you, saying, 'I repent,' you shall forgive him."
-Luke 17:1-4 NKJV™

"When angry, do not sin; do not ever let your wrath (your exasperation, your fury or indignation) last until the sun goes down. Leave no [such] room or foothold for the devil [give no opportunity to him]." -Ephesians 4:26-27AMP

"Let all bitterness and indignation and wrath (passion, rage, bad temper) and resentment (anger, animosity) and quarreling (brawling, clamor, contention) and slander (evil-speaking, abusive or blasphemous language) be banished from you, with all malice (spite, ill will, or baseness of any kind). And become useful and helpful and kind to one another, tenderhearted (compassionate, understanding, loving-hearted), forgiving one another [readily and freely], as God in Christ forgave you."
-Ephesians 4:31-32 AMP

POETIC INSIGHT:

As sure as we live, we will be offended. Someone, somewhere will do or say something that brings feelings of resentment and anger. As Christian believers, we are challenged to handle offense in such a way that our response makes the offense impotent – unable to produce the rage, hatred and malice that is waiting in the wings for its cue to take center stage. Nothing good can come from these negative emotions.

WALK OUT THE WORD:

The feelings that result from an offense can be overwhelming. Whenever you are offended, try to remember that God has great hearing and excellent vision. He heard what was said and saw what was done. He also knows the motives behind the actions, motives we can't always determine at first glance. Rest assured that the action of the offender did not go unnoticed by our Heavenly Father.

In the same manner, try to remember that he can also hear your response and see your reactions. And, he knows your motives as well. Purpose to be still when you are offended. Take a moment to "cool off."Ask God to fight your battle on your behalf and to help you to respond appropriately.

GREAT EXPECTATIONS

God's thoughts are greater than mine
So I have to elevate my way of thinking
Revelation gave Peter faith to walk on water
But reasoning caused him to start sinking

I'm seated in Heavenly places with Christ Jesus
I look down on problems from Christ's point of view
Heavenly perspective assures me
God will do everything He said He would do

His word cannot return unto Him void
It must accomplish its intended task
So I speak His truth in faith and with wisdom
Expecting every word to come to pass

I expect to have life abundantly
With God's angels keeping charge
I expect to never be forsaken
To awaken to new mercies every dawn

I expect a life of manifestation
I'm in the palace, can't think like a peasant
No fear of lack, the King's my daddy
And He rules all of earth and heaven

I don't give credence to circumstances
That are based only on facts
What is seen is temporary
Why should I base my life on that?

What God says is so
As seen in his word is what I believe
My faith is strong, not impotent
And promises are delivered to me

LIVING WATER:

"In the morning, O LORD, you hear my voice; in the morning I lay my requests before you and wait in expectation." –Psalm 5:3 NKJV™

*"For my thoughts are not your thoughts, neither are your ways my ways,"
declares the LORD. As the heavens are higher than the earth, so are my
ways higher than your ways and my thoughts than your thoughts. As the
rain and the snow come down from heaven, and do not return to it without
watering the earth and making it bud and flourish, so that it yields seed for
the sower and bread for the eater, so is my word that goes out from my
mouth: It will not return to me empty, but will accomplish what I desire and
achieve the purpose for which I sent it. You will go out in joy and be led
forth in peace; the mountains and hills will burst into song before you,
and all the trees of the field will clap their hands. Instead of the thornbush
will grow the pine tree, and instead of briers the myrtle will grow. This will
be for the LORD's renown, for an everlasting sign, which will not be
destroyed."* –Isaiah 55:8-13 NKJV™

POETIC INSIGHT:

Great, small, or nothing at all, you will get what you expect! That's a
principle of God's kingdom and it's true.

WALK OUT THE WORD:

Write down one thing you expect to obtain in your life. Find a scripture to
support your expectation. Every day for the next week, ask God to help you
align your expectation with your faith and read your supporting scripture
daily. Continue until you have what you expect.

Here's an example:
Expectation/Need: Peace of mind.
Supporting Scripture: *"For God has not given us a spirit of fear, but of
power and of love and of a sound mind."* -2Timothy 1:7
Request to God: *Dear Lord, Thank you for your presence. Right now, my
life is chaotic; I worry a lot and I am not clear headed. I don't have peace.
Your word says you have given me a sound mind. Help me to change my
perspective to yours and help me to begin to expect to receive the sound
mind your promised. I can't do this without you and I know you will help
me. In Jesus Name, Amen.*

NOW AND AT ONCE

Right now all that God spoke over me is my reality
Tomorrow is no guarantee and yesterday has already become all it could
ever be
Now and at once I live a life of endless wonderful possibilities
For Elohim, El-Shaddai, Jehovah-Jireh, Jehovah Rapha, Jehovah-Nissi,
Jehovah Shalom, I Am that I Am, Providence, Yahweh is for me
Jesus the Christ is with me, and the Holy Spirit is in me
Right now I have faith as a mustard seed
So nothing is impossible for me, for you see
Right now I can do all things through Christ who strengthens me
Right now I seek first the Kingdom of God and His righteousness
Knowing all things I need are added unto me
I take no thought for my life, I don't worry, I don't stress
Right now I love the Lord my God first and foremost
With all my strength, mind, soul, and heart
Right now I love my neighbors as myself
The just and unjust, for the wheat and tares grow together
And Christ shall pull them apart
Right now I pray without ceasing, I praise God constantly
Right now I worship God in Spirit and Truth, I worship Him only
My relationship with God is the most intimate and top priority
Right now the peace of God that surpasses all understanding
Accompanies me everywhere I go
Like a river the joy in my heart overflows
Right now I make a joyful noise unto the Lord
I serve Jesus with gladness and I come before His presence
Singing a new song
Right now in my weakness His strength is perfect, my Lord is strong
Right now Jesus Christ is my strong tower, my fortress, my refuge
A very present help in trouble, my peace, my guide, my keeper, my shield
Right now God teaches my hands to war, and my fingers to fight
Right now I am victorious no matter where the battlefield
Right now no weapon formed against me shall prosper
For I am more than a conquer
And greater is He that is within me
Then He that is within the world
For He that is within me has already overcome the world
Right now in every arena of life I rule and reign
For I am a king and priest with God given authority
Where I step becomes my kingdom
For I've been granted dominion over all the earth
Over the fowls of the air, and the fish of the sea
Right now I humbly follow Jesus Christ and the leadership

Of those who He has given authority over me
Right now I submit to and support the vision of my head
Even when there are parts of the vision that I don't see
I choose this day to serve the Lord my God not mammon
As for me and my house this is the decision I make
I am not a tyrant over those whom I rule,
But a servant governing with God's love
For to be great,
Matthew 20:26 declares the route of the servant
Is the route you must take
Right now I mortify and put to death all the desires of my flesh
Right now I confess all my sins and repent
Right now Jesus Christ forgives me from my sins
And cleanses me from all unrighteousness
Right now I count it all joy when I go through
Various trails and temptations
Right now when I am tempted, I immediately take
God's provided way of escape
So that I am able to bear it when I face temptations
Right now I resist the devil and he flees from me
I absolutely refuse to give place to Satan
Right now I flee sexual immorality
Right now I am in Christ Jesus
So over me there is no condemnation
God is not the author of confusion
Right now I cast down imaginations and every high thing
That exalts itself against the knowledge of God
Right now I bring into captivity every thought
To the obedience of Christ
Right now I am faithful and stable in all my ways
There is no doubt in my heart, in me there is no double-mindedness
Right now I receive, live, operate in, give, and demonstrate
A life of unconditional forgiveness
Right now my heart is Christ like,
My heart absolutely refuses to hold, house, carry, hide, receive and/or entertain
Unjust anger, lust, envy, jealously, malice, strife, gossip, fear, false theology,
Pride, revenge, idols, rage, doubt, disobedience, unforgiveness, selfishness
Greed, covetousness, confusion, stress, or bitterness
Right now all generational curses and ungodly mentalities
Have been broken, destroyed, and removed forever
From me and my bloodline
Poverty, sickness, lack, and disease can no longer
Touch me or anything that is mine
Right now God is the strength of my heart and my portion forever
Right now I trust in the Lord, so I am like Mount Zion

Which cannot be shaken but endures forever
Right now wisdom is my sister
Understanding is my nearest kin
And I give attention to know her
That her secrets I might win
Right now I take firm hold of instruction
Right now I love and keep wisdom
I embrace and exalt understanding, I do not let them go
I abide in Jesus Christ and His words abide in me
Right now His words are in the midst of my heart and sets it aglow
Right now I guard my heart with all diligence
For out of my heart the issues of life flow

Right now it is not all about my gifts, my call, my anointing or ministry
Right now my life is not even about me
It is about seeing Christ in all aspects
For when the Father shows me Christ, I be what I see
Right now I suffer long and I am kind
I do not envy
I do not parade myself or puff myself up
Right now I do not behave unseemly
Right now I don't seek my own will
I am not easily provoked
I thinkest no evil
Right now I do not boast
For I am not proud or vain
I do not hurt or mislead others
In efforts of vain glory and/or self gain
Right now I don't rejoice in iniquity
I rejoice only in the truth
Right now I hopeth all things, believeth all things and beareth
All things no matter what they may be
I also endureth all things
1 Corinthians chapter 13 declares these truths about me
Right now I have a revelation of Christ as God's perfected love
I say, when I look at Christ, Love is what I see
So right now I am Charity

Right now I delight myself in the Lord
And He gives me the desires of my heart
When I pray I believe I receive my heart's desires
I don't waver from this belief
Even when tested by Red Seas, Lion's dens, and furnace fires
Right now I walk in the Spirit
So that I don't fulfill the lust of the flesh
I am not under the law because my life
Is a life in which the fruits of the Spirit manifest

Right now I walk by faith
Not by what I see or feel
For right now by the stripes of Jesus Christ I am healed
Right now it is my season to bring forth fruit
My root system has been established and I am like a tree
Planted by the rivers of water, everything I do shall prosper
And be for God's Glory
For right now I experience total life prosperity
Right now I operate with a Kingdom mentality
Right now the covenant promises God made with Abraham and his seed
Are promises God has established with me
Today I chose life, I fear the Lord, and God helps me
To keep all His commandments, and walk in His ways
Which means I receive and walk in all the provisions of the Abraham
covenant currently
Right now I am completely debt free
I am God's servant
And right now He delights in my prosperity
I am a cheerful giver and I sow bountifully
Therefore I reap bountifully
Right now into my bosom men give unto me
Right now I receive good measure, pressed down, shaken together
And running over because Luke 6:38 says that's how it is to be
Right now my wealth is not threaten by the trouble of the world's economy
Right now every gift and talent God put inside of me
Causes streams of income to flow back into me
Which means that I am constantly flooded with currency
Right now I ask for and expect money from unexpected sources
So you see, right now unexpected sources are delivering money to me
Matthew 7:7 and John 15:7 lets us know that asking is the key
Right now Father God in the name of Jesus the Christ
I ask that above all Your provisions and prosperity
That You make it a priority
To do whatever necessary
To keep me from becoming like those described
In the 19th verse of the 8th chapter of Deuteronomy
Right now even though I am one of the richest entrepreneurs in history
Considered so because of my abundance
Of houses, banks, businesses, investments, intellectual property,
Capital and other assets, for I could afford to buy whole countries
That's right, entire lands
None of this will cause me to forget the Lord my God
Right now I seek God's face more than His hands
Because right now I understand
That I am like a holy UPS
A distribution system through which all nations of the world will be blessed
Yes, through finances

But more importantly they are blessed
As I introduce them to and train them up
In the ways of the God of love and righteousness
Right now I walk with God like Enoch in Genesis
Right now I obey God completely, without question, and without hesitation
Right now God is using me to bless generations
Right now my family and my family to be
Is saved, filled with the Holy Spirit, walks in obedience and forgiveness
And spread the love of Christ to all whom they see
Right now my wife
Is a virtuous, beautiful woman who fears God
Walks in faith and purity
Has a great sense of humor
And loves me for me
However her love for me
Is outweighed by her love for the Holy Trinity
Right now God is teaching me to be
A Christian son, brother, husband, father, friend
As well as a minister, teacher, student, and businessman
I do not agree with temporary facts
That speaks of situations being dead and dry
For God has commanded
Again I say to you prophesy
Right now I stand on my feet and declare eternal truth
Wind, right now and at once I command you
To carry this whole prophecy throughout the sky
Angels, go forth and make these things occur immediately
For the Word of God says if I declare a thing
It will be established unto me
As it was with Paul in 2 Corinthians 3:3
The Spirit of God speaks through me manifestly
God's word cannot return to Him void
For God cannot lie
Right now, in the name of Jesus the Christ
All these things I have spoken
Are established in Heaven
And they are established, manifested, and revealed
In my life on Earth
Because the moment I spoke
I gave it birth!

LIVING WATER:

"Then Caleb quieted the people before Moses, and said, "Let us go up at once and take possession, for we are well able to overcome it."
–Numbers 13:30 NKJV™

"You will make your prayer to Him, and He will hear you, and you will pay your vows. You shall also decide and decree a thing, and it shall be established for you; and the light [of God's favor] shall shine upon your ways. When they make [you] low, you will say, [There is] a lifting up; and the humble person He lifts up and saves. He will even deliver the one [for whom you intercede] who is not innocent; yes, he will be delivered through the cleanness of your hands." -Job 22:27-30 AMP

POETIC INSIGHT:

Tomorrow is not guaranteed, and yesterday cannot be changed. Now is all you have. Your "now" may be less than what you want. I challenge you to employ the principle of speaking life to your situations. Death and life are in the power of the tongue and they that love it shall eat the fruit thereof. Your words have power.

WALK OUT THE WORD:

Open your mouth and declare what your "now" will be!

THE WALK

The first step felt strange
A rush of excitement coursed my veins
As I opened my mind to the possibilities
I immediately felt uncertainty

Voices hissed in the distance
"You don't know what you're getting into"
"It's never been done, it can't be done"
"I wouldn't try that if I were you"

Step two

Somehow I'm gaining confidence
Despite all the negativity
Must concentrate on the other voice I hear
Calling me into my destiny

Step three

Focused more on where I'm going
There must be good in store
Must think about future successes
And leave my past on the other side of the door

Step four

Only God could open this door
To a fascinating new world where dreams thrive
I am starting to achieve things, great and small
Fear and doubt are beginning to die

Step five

But here comes the test
I feel a slight chill across my chest
Winds of adversity begin to blow
And I second guess what I already know
Dread darkens my journey
I make a list of my inadequacies
I'm scared to turn because then I'll see
Those I left behind watching me
They'll see me sink in this new thing I tried
They will criticize, I want to run and hide

It seems God is nowhere to be found
"Lord save me! I'm going down!"
"It was at your word that I even attempted this
But there's no way out and I'm in a terrible fix."

Step six

Jesus steps forward and stretches out His hand
"O you of little faith, why did you doubt?"
He catches me and pulls me out
With His strength I am able to stand again

Step Seven

The lesson here is simple
You must experience faith firsthand
Don't worry about the critics
Those left behind will never understand
Walk and talk with God
Do exactly what He is calling you to do
Don't let fear lead to disobedience
Trust the Master to take every step with you

LIVING WATER:

"And straightway Jesus constrained his disciples to get into a ship, and to go before him unto the other side, while he sent the multitudes away. And when he had sent the multitudes away, he went up into a mountain apart to pray: and when the evening was come, he was there alone. But the ship was now in the midst of the sea, tossed with waves: for the wind was contrary. And in the fourth watch of the night Jesus went unto them, walking on the sea. And when the disciples saw him walking on the sea, they were troubled, saying, It is a spirit; and they cried out for fear. But straightway Jesus spake unto them, saying, Be of good cheer; it is I; be not afraid. And Peter answered him and said, Lord if it be thou, bid me come unto thee on the water. And he said, Come. And Peter was come down out of the ship, he walked on the water, to go to Jesus. But when he saw the wind boisterous, he was afraid; and beginning to sink, he cried, saying, Lord, save me. And immediately Jesus stretched forth his hand, and caught him, and said unto him, O thou of little faith, wherefore didst thou doubt? And when they were come into the ship, the wind ceased. Then they that were in the ship came and worshiped him saying, Of a truth thou art the Son of God." -Matthew 14:22-33 KJV

POETIC INSIGHT:

Do you trust God? How much? In the 14th chapter of Matthew, when Jesus said "come," he did not say "Peter come." All the disciples heard the command but only one stepped out of the boat. Jesus offered them an experience that would change their lives and their testimonies forever, but only one was willing to trust God enough to move in the direction of His voice. All of the disciples boarded the boat to go to the other side as Jesus had instructed, but in the mist of obeying Jesus they refuse to heed His call into an unconventional way to cross the sea... by walking.

In this story, Peter is often criticized for sinking in the ocean after getting frightened. But, we must remember that Peter had the faith to take the first and most difficult step – the step out of the comfort and predictability of the boat.

Any step of faith will be challenged by naysayers and people who let their opportunity at a faith walk pass them by. Not every naysayer will mean you harm. Some are fellow believers or people who love you and do not want to see you get hurt. But, if God has issued a call in your life, don't stand still. Take the first step, then the next. Don't ever let people love you out of your destiny.

WALK OUT THE WORD:

What is it that you know God is calling you to do? Is He calling you to start a business; to sing a song; to write a book; to write a play; to move into another career; to leave a relationship; to start a relationship; to go back to school; to forgive someone; to help someone, to take a vacation, to start a family, to spend more time with Him? Stop trying to decide if you will be able to do what God is calling you to do and decide to trust him. (What's in your hand Moses?)

He is calling you... will you come? His hand is stretched out to you... will you take it?

"I tell you the truth, if anyone says to this mountain, 'Go, throw yourself into the sea,' and does not doubt in his heart but believes that what he says will happen, it will be done for him.

Mark 11:23 NIV

WE'VE GOT SOME BRIGHTER DAYS AHEAD...

Faith handed his newborn daughter to his wife
Love wrapped her arms around their first child
"Let's name her Hope," Faith said
Love nodded yes and smiled
"IT'S A GIRL!!!" yelled Faith
Faith looked at his wife
"Love," he said, *"I am so proud*
Not just of my precious daughter,
I'm also proud of you
My wonderful wife and Hope's beautiful mother"
Tears of joy leapt from Love's face
She and Faith burst into praise
Thanking God for the blessing that had taken place
"We have endured so much," Faith said
Love replied, *"There were times*
When I didn't think we could take it."
"Me too," said Faith, *"But now that we have Hope,*
We have to make it!!!"
Faith held his daughter and hugged his wife
As they began to reminisce...
From the moment that
Faith and Love had their first kiss
Both knew that neither
Had ever felt like this
Their feelings grew strong
The courtship was amazing
Faith got on one knee
Love accepted the ring
They exchange vows
In a ceremony fit for royalty
He cherished her as his queen
She honored him as her king
They agreed to submit to God
And allow His word and perfect will
To rule everything
In their lives and household
In Love, Faith had found a virtuous woman
Her value is higher than rubies
Her wisdom more precious than gold...
They reminisced on the ups and downs
The triumphs and attacks
The blows of life that had been designed
To make them give up and turn them back

They thought on how they prayed and praised
Determined to stick to it
And no matter what they faced
God brought them through it
Yes, God brought them through
And now they knew...why
Because there was a new Hope
That would be birthed on the other side...
Faith held baby Hope high in the air
"She has your pretty smile," he told his wife
Love grinned and said, *"She has her daddy's good hair"*
Faith handed Hope to her mother
Got down on his knees and prayed this prayer:
"Father God thank you for this day
And for the Hope that you have given to me and my wife
This great gift in this little package
Has change my entire life
Help me and Love to please you in all that we do
Father we dedicate our new Hope to you!"
Faith stood on his feet and held Love by her hand
Looked her in the eyes and said, *"Understand,*
I am an even more dedicated and committed man
With Love by my side and new Hope in my heart
I know that I can stand!!!
We will pursue our lives with renewed purpose and passion
We won't just talk about our goals and dreams
We will take God directed actions"
Faith and Love held baby Hope close
As they sat side by side
For hours they prayed and praised
They laugh and cried
The spoke of the brighter days ahead
How their latter would be greater
And how the best was yet to come
Faith and Love thank each other
For the new Hope they had been given
And their hearts overflowed with joy
As they thought of the impact
Baby Hope would have on the life they are living
Faith told Love how beautiful she is
And Love told him how
He would never know what those words were worth
And this is the story of how an unwavering Faith and enduring Love
Impacted the whole earth
Because when Faith and Love are united
Hope will be birthed ...

TRANSLATION...

We have some brighter days ahead
We have days filled with laughter
We have days overflowing with joy and cheer
We have days of quality time with those we hold dear
We have days of perfected love casting out fear
We have days of healing, wholeness, and great health
We have days of understanding the true meaning of wealth
We have days of enjoying riches and prosperity
We have days of the blind being able to see
We have days of debt cancellation
We have days of credit restoration
We have days of family reconciliation
We have days of peace in the land
We have days of giving helping hands
We have days of worshiping God and not man
We have days of emotional stability
We have days of home cook meals and
large glasses of the sweetest iced tea
We have days of friends being true
We have days of getting encouragement out of the blue
We have days of respecting one another
We have days of different races learning to love each other
We have days of getting answers to our prayers
We have days when happiness is the only reason for tears
We have days of enemies becoming footstools
We have days when children's innocence is protected
and no child rushes to be grown
We have days of careers that we love and businesses that we own
We have days of not working while on vacation
We have days of being able to go home for relaxation
We have days of passion being balance with purity
We have days when desperation leads spouses to the alter
And not to infidelity
We have days of no longer living selfishly
But instead humbling ourselves and giving God the glory
We have days that are purpose driven
We days of life being worth living
We have some brighter days ahead
No matter what you hear or see
No matter how dim your current situation may be
Listen to me
We, both you and me, have some brighter days ahead
For you see
When the love of God and faith in God is combined
Hope comes from that unity

When babies are born they announce their presence with a cry
The "Wah Wah" let's everyone know that they are alive
So I want you to think of every situation and circumstance
That makes you worry, stress, frightened, and causes you to cry
And declare, "WE HAVE SOME BRIGHTER DAYS AHEAD!!!"
Then hold your head up high
And the next time the tears begin to fall from your eyes
Let it be a reminder that you are indeed alive
And so is the small bundle of Hope that was birthed on the inside

LIVING WATER:

"And now abide faith, hope, love, these three; but the greatest of these is love." -1 Corinthians 13:13 NKJV™

"For I know the thoughts that I think toward you, says the LORD, thoughts of peace and not of evil, to give you a future and a hope." -Jeremiah 29:11 NKJV™

POETIC INSIGHT:

It's not over until God says it's over. Love fuels faith. Faith is the substance of things hoped for. So you can have faith but if you are not hoping for anything...what's the point?

Listen, when a woman is pregnant we say that she is expecting. She is not wishing for a baby or thinking maybe it will happen. She is expecting. She has a calm and confident assurance that a baby will be born even though she cannot see the baby. Preparations are made for the arrival of the baby. When her water breaks and the labor pains begin, the trial may be intense. But, the promise is on the other side of the push. Seeing the baby makes it all worthwhile.

When people come against your vision, goals and dreams and you hurt and cry, please know that your water just broke and your pain is that of labor. Let God hold your hand and listen for His voice to let you know when to PUSH!

WALK OUT THE WORD:

Get alone with God and give voice to what you've been hoping for.

WOMEN OF PURPOSE

God never makes mistakes
He makes masterpieces
Water was never intended to be dry
Grass was never intended to be blue
And I guarantee every woman,
That God knew
Exactly what He was doing when He made you
God knew your date of birth
Before He made the earth
His fingerprints are all over you
Because it was God's hands that formed you
From the young and sassy
To the elderly and classy
From the not so small to the very thin
No matter your shade of skin
You are all cherished
Because never again
Will the world be blessed with someone just like you
You have a divine destiny
Something no one else will be able to do
Honor and strength are the fabrics
From which your clothing is made
Wisdom resides in you
And the light of your love never fades
Through the woman came the birth of nations
YOU are God's creation
God made the sun and the moon
God made hills and mountains
Oh, how majestic He is!
God has the power to make
The stars in the sky
As well as the beautiful face
That surrounds your eyes
How awesome God must be
To make rivers and lakes
And even greater still
Is the fact that God doesn't make mistakes
The Master makes Pieces that are priceless

LIVING WATER:

"For I know the thoughts that I think toward you, says the LORD, thoughts of peace and not of evil, to give you a future and a hope." -Jeremiah 29:11 NKJV™

"Many daughters have done well, But you excel them all." Charm is deceitful and beauty is passing, But a woman who fears the LORD, she shall be praised." -Proverbs 31: 29-30 NKJV™

"Go, gather all the Jews who are present in Shushan, and fast for me; neither eat nor drink for three days, night or day. My maids and I will fast likewise. And so I will go to the king, which is against the law; and if I perish, I perish!" Esther 4:16 NKJV™

POETIC INSIGHT:

Women are sometimes undervalued by society. Everyday there are women who are abused by their husbands and/or disrespected by their children. Some women are made to feel poorly about themselves if they don't have a husband or child. Many women are still paid less money for doing the same level work as a man and dehumanized as sexual objects.

However, regardless of what society says, you are who God says you are. Every single woman is handcrafted by God. Stop calling yourself ugly, fat, or stupid. Stop thinking that you are not smart enough or pretty enough. You don't have to give up your integrity or purity. Stop thinking the abuse was your fault. No, you did not deserve to be cheated on. Don't be afraid to go after your dreams. God knows exactly who you are and he loves you as you are.

WALK OUT THE WORD:

It is so dangerous to compare ourselves with others. When we make comparisons, we either become bitter, downcast or prideful. You are God's unique creation. Love and accept the woman you are today. Men, share this with the women in your life that you love and respect.

HIGHLY EXALTED

The Lion from Judah's Tribe
Can you hear His roar
In your spirit? Yes, He's still alive

The Salvation of the Lord is here
Praise Him now
Evil imaginations are cast down

Elevate your praise today
He's high
High and Lifted Up
Elevate

The Wonderful Counselor
The Living Water
Author & Finisher
Soul Redeemer

Perfect love casteth out fear
Look towards the hills
Help has arrived... Child, just be still

Praise is a step in the direction of breakthrough
The High Priest knows your suffering
The Bread of Life longs to nourish you
The Judge wants to grant liberty
To you, Yes, you can be freed

Elevate your praise today
He's high
High and Lifted Up
Elevate

LIVING WATER:

A HYMN OF PRAISE
*And in that day you will say: "O LORD, I will praise You; Though You were
angry with me, Your anger is turned away, and You comfort me. Behold,
God is my salvation, I will trust and not be afraid; 'For YAH, the LORD, is my
strength and song; He also has become my salvation.'" Therefore with joy*

you will draw water From the wells of salvation. And in that day you will say: "Praise the LORD, call upon His name; Declare His deeds among the peoples, Make mention that His name is exalted. Sing to the LORD, For He has done excellent things; This is known in all the earth. Cry out and shout, O inhabitant of Zion, For great is the Holy One of Israel in your midst!"
- Isaiah 12:1-6 NKJV™

POETIC INSIGHT:

This poem is written as a song of praise to God. There is victory in our praise. Satan led worship in heaven before he revolted against God and was kicked out. Now, he attempts to keep us from doing what he once had the honor of doing – praising God. Let nothing keep you from praising God.

WALK OUT THE WORD:

Sing unto God. Get a song in your heart for Him and sing it to him throughout the day.

VICTORIOUS

The Lion of the Tribe of Judah has conquered
The True Vine is flourishing
The Prince of Peace reigns
The Servant is now Master over everything

The Light of the World prevails
The Redeemer rescues souls
The Chief Cornerstone has been established
Emmanuel is in control

The Anchor is secure
The Judge grants liberty
The Bread of Life fulfills
The Living Water flows freely

Life is what The Rock gives
The Dayspring disperses fear
The Prophet is interceding
The Man of Sorrows dries tears

The Messiah has been manifested
The Resurrection has been revealed
The Word is immutable
The High Priest knows how suffering feels

The Wonderful Counselor is all powerful
The Alpha & Omega is true
The Carpenter builds masterpieces
The Mediator made an everlasting breakthrough

Faithful is The Author & Finisher
Sovereign is The Holy One
We cannot be defeated
Because the Only Begotten Son has won

All hail the power of His name!
The King of Kings, the Lord Jesus
Because of the finished work of Christ
We are eternally victorious!

LIVING WATER:

"For in him dwelleth all the fulness of the Godhead bodily. And ye are complete in him, which is the head of all principality and power:....And having spoiled principalities and powers, he made a show of them openly, triumphing over them in it." -Colossians 2:9-10, 15 KJV

"For I am persuaded, that neither death, nor life, nor angels, nor principalities, nor powers, nor things present, nor things to come, Nor height, nor depth, nor any other creature, shall be able to separate us from the love of God, which is in Christ Jesus our Lord." -Romans 8:38-39 KJV

"And Jesus came and spake unto them, saying, All power is given unto me in heaven and in earth." -Matthew 28:18 KJV

POETIC INSIGHT:

Believe the truth of God's word. When it is all said and done, we overcome every enemy. We win!

WALK OUT THE WORD:

Listen to something that makes you feel victorious. Remember, faith comes by hearing and hearing by the word of God. May I make a few suggestions?

- "Victory" – Yolanda Adams
- "The Champion" – Carmen
- "Awesome God" – Rich Mullins or Kirk Franklin
- "Revelation Song" – Kari Jobe
- "Victory" – Tye Tribbett & GA

WHEN I SAY...

When I say, "I love you"
There is so much I'm trying to convey
Here are some of the things I mean
When "I love you" are the words I say
I *love* the way you make ME feel
I *love* the way you make ME laugh
I *love* the way you stand up on MY behalf
I *love* how the best in ME is what you see
I *love* how you give of yourself to ME so willingly
Truly, I *love* you, Yes, I really do
Or, at least I thought I did
Until I found out that love is suppose to be about YOU
When I reflect on the actions of Jesus because of His love for me
And meditate on the characteristics of love found in the B-I-B-L-E
My eyes have been open and now my heart can see
That my previous declarations of love for you
Were really
Self centered proclamations of how much
I was enjoying my selfish reality
But today is a new day
And when I say, "I love you"
There is a new message I'm trying to convey
Here are some of the things I mean
When, "I love you" are the words I say
I love YOU for who YOU are
I love YOU despite of who YOU are not
I love YOU for who YOU are becoming
Not for what YOU got
I'm saying that I will support YOU
When it is inconvenient to me
I will sacrifice for YOUR success
And never seek any of the glory
I love YOU means I respect and cherish YOU
I value YOU as a person
And not because of the things YOU do
Me loving YOU means that
I show YOU patience and kindness
That I rejoice at YOUR happiness,
Instead of being envious
And that I don't abandon YOU when YOU are in distress
When I say I love YOU
I'm saying I exalt YOU higher than me
And that's the way its suppose to be

Because, when I say, "I love you"
For it to really be true
It can't be about me

LIVING WATER:

"Love suffers long and is kind; love does not envy; love does not parade itself, is not puffed up; does not behave rudely, does not seek its own, is not provoked, thinks no evil; does not rejoice in iniquity, but rejoices in the truth; bears all things, believes all things, hopes all things, endures all things." -1 Corinthians 13:4-7 NKJV™

POETIC INSIGHT:

"Take a moment and read 1 Corinthians 13:1-13. Pick a different attribute of love each week. Put each attribute into practice. Seek to love according to the attributes of love as noted in the scripture.

WALK OUT THE WORD:

You will never be perfect in love. As believers, we are being perfected in love, but only God's love is perfect because God is love. Thank him today for His love that is unconditional and unfailing.

> (GREATER THAN)

God is greater than your problems
Greater than your past
Greater than your hurt
From relationships that didn't last

God is greater than your fears
Greater than your failures
Greater than family and friends
Greater than enemies on their worst behavior

You may feel *less than* able
To live life abundantly
But if He has been *added* to your life
Greater is your destiny

Speak to your day
Like placing an order with a waiter
Then offer a shout of praise, because
The God we serve is Greater

LIVING WATER:

"Ye are of God, little children, and have overcome them: because greater is he that is in you, than he that is in the world." -1 JOHN 4:4 KJV

POETIC INSIGHT:

No matter what tries to subtract (-) from your life, if you add (+) Jesus and not allow anything to divide you (÷) from Him then you will find that your joy, blessings and abilities are multiplied (x) and that Christ in you makes you greater than (>) than anything the world will bring your way.

WALK OUT THE WORD:

Encourage yourself in the Lord by remembering the ways in which he's shown himself strong in your life.

Verily, verily, I say unto you, He that believeth on me, the works that I do shall he do also; and greater works than these shall he do; because I go unto my Father.

And whatsoever ye shall ask in my name, that will I do, that the Father may be glorified in the Son.

John 14:12-13 KJV

SO WHAT

So what if you sold your body for money
On more than one occasion
So what if you keep the weed blazing
So what if you steal everything in sight
So what if you always starting fights
So what if you got a foul mouth
So what if you sexing everything that moves
So what if you in the club jamming to the latest groove
So what if you are hooked up in pornography
So what if you got tattoos and rings piercing your body
So what if the taste of alcohol you just can't let go
So what if you do things just for show
So what if you tell lies everyday
So what if you were the one who pulled the trigger
So what if your ride is bigger
So what if crack residue is on your floor
So what if you've been in church pretending
So what if your body odor is offending
So what if you spending your days
Doing things to waste your life away
So what if you're in prison
So what if you've dropped out of school
So what if you act like a fool
So what if you have made some mistakes
So what if no one ever gives you a break
So what if your heart was broken
So what if you're addicted to food
So what if self gratification is the only thing you can think of
To put you in a better mood
So what if you had a baby before marriage
Or did stuff to your body hoping for a miscarriage
So what if your decisions has caused you
To be caught up in something you can't see your way through
So what if church folks have judged and condemned you
So what if I or anyone else claiming to represent God disapproves of you
If we do, sounds like we have our own love and forgiveness issues to work
through
Because not only did Jesus die for us, He died for all of you
It doesn't matter how "dirty", "nasty", or "bad" you have been
Or the evil and wickedness you are currently into
Jesus is waiting with his arms open wide to forgive you
Yes, accepting Jesus Christ as Lord is the only way to escape Hell
But there are so many benefits that we Christians fail to tell

You
Why?
Sadly, because we are too busy acting holier than thou
So that we can criticize you
But it is right there in John 3:16-18
God loves you
And He doesn't expect you to get "clean"
Before coming to Him
He knows all about your life and He will accept you no matter how grim
The details may be
In Christ we are promised peace, hope,
Strength, joy, love, forgiveness, and prosperity
For who the son sets free, is free indeed
And Jesus came that we might have life and have it more abundantly
It's not about trying to be "good" so you can go to heaven some day
It is about ruling and reigning this day
For we are Kings and Priests, and life and death are in the things we say
So I apologize if the church folks have judged or condemned you
Truth is... we have done (and at times unfortunately still do)
Things worse than anything you could even think to do
So I state these things to bring the truth to you
Now you know that no matter what you have done
Jesus is waiting to love, forgive, and bless you
I've just got one question:
So what are you going to do?

LIVING WATER:

"For God so loved the world that He gave His only begotten Son, that whosoever believeth in him should not perish, but have everlasting life. For God sent not his Son into the world to condemn the world; but that the world through him might be saved.
He that believeth on him is not condemned: but he that believeth not is condemned already, because he hath not believed in the name of the only begotten Son of God." -John 3:16-18 KJV

"That if you will confess with your mouth the Lord Jesus, and shall believe in you heart that God hath raised him from the dead, you shall be saved." -Romans 10:9 KJV

POETIC INSIGHT:

"Just as I am" is the name of a popular hymn. However it is more than that...it is truth! No matter who you are and no matter what you have done, God is willing and wanting to forgive you.

In the beginning, God and Adam, the first man enjoyed a close relationship. But when Adam sinned and disobeyed God, the result was death. Not only would Adam and all mankind die physically, mankind became separated from God – a spiritual death. Man's close relationship with God was lost and every person thereafter would be born into sin. All mankind entered a "fallen" state of being. (See Genesis Chapters 1 – 3)

Mankind was instructed to offer animal sacrifices to make atonement for their sins. But this did not solve the dilemma of eternal separation from God. God does not want to be separated from us. So, God sent Jesus, His only begotten son to earth to become our lasting sacrifice and savior. Through a miraculous birth, Jesus was conceived by the Holy Spirit in a virgin named Mary. Because Jesus was born of a woman and of the Holy Spirit, he was fully God and fully man. Jesus lived without sin.

Because Jesus was without sin He was able to become the sacrifice that would make atonement for the sins of all of mankind. Jesus paid our sin debt in full. He did this by willingly dying on the cross for all of our sins (past, present and future). (See Matthew Chapters 1,2,27)

After three days God raised Jesus from the dead as the first born of many brethren. Jesus ascended into heaven and now sits at the right hand of God the Father where He intercedes on our behalf. When we accept Jesus Christ as our Lord and Savior, what we are saying is that we acknowledge that we are sinners and that we accept the payment that Jesus made on our behalf. (See Matthew Chapter 28)

When we accept what God sent Jesus to do for us this allows us to be reconnected (have our relationship restored) to God. By having our relationship restored with God through acceptance of Jesus Christ we access eternal life with God. If we don't accept what Jesus Christ did for us than that means our sin debt has not been satisfied. Those who will not accept Jesus as their savior will be held personally responsible for their sins – which is a price no man can pay.

Since Jesus was the only one capable of paying sins cost, those who do not accept Jesus Christ will remain separated from God for eternity. The good news for us is that God wants to have a personal relationship with us and that it doesn't matter what we have done. God knows all about you and He loves you so much that He used Jesus Christ as a way for you to be forgiven and reconnected to Him. (See Romans Chapter 10; 1 John Chapter 1)

WALK OUT THE WORD:

Perhaps you are reading this and you have not received Christ's salvation. When Jesus died on the cross for our sins, he made salvation available to anyone who would receive him and believe in him. You can have salvation this day by believing the words of this prayer and reciting it aloud:

"Lord Jesus, I am a sinner and I stand in need. I come to you in prayer to ask for the salvation that you made available through your death on the cross. I believe God raised you from the dead and I confess that you are Lord. Please come into my heart and lead me forward in your will. It's in your name I pray, amen."

If you prayed this prayer, according to Romans 10:9, you are saved! Congratulations!

I suggest that you purchase a Holy Bible; consider a version (wording) of the Bible that you can easily understand. Then, begin attending a Bible-believing church to help you grow in your faith.

HOMECOMING

The stench is unbearable
The wind slaps him in the face
Tears roll from his eyes
He is ashamed and disgraced
The party is long over
All his money is gone
His friends for life have scattered
Leaving him all alone
He was once favored
And lived a life that was blessed
Now he is empty
Now he is distressed
He made poor choices
Thought he knew all he needed to know
Could do what he wanted
Now, he has nothing to left show
But pain and regret
His pride tries to overlook his mistakes
But his hunger won't let him forget
How he insisted on living life his way
By his own rules
Now a high price he has to pay
For traveling the way of fools
He is in a foreign land
He is dirty, sweaty and alone
Feeding pigs that are eating better than him
"Is that a husk from some old corn?"
He contemplates a meal of complacency and mediocrity
"Feast or famine?"
Whispers the enemy
But the young man sees through the deception
He says, "This could never satisfy me
I was seated at a table, where I was considered royalty
Even my father's hired servants have plenty
I must humble myself and plead for a servant's mercy"
He comes to himself, turns his face toward home
His father sees him coming and meets him on the road
Runs to his son, hugs and kiss
The son is not expecting to be received like this
"Son, I give a *Thank You* and *An Ode to God*
Because of *The Promise* that
If you train up a child...When they are old they will not depart.
This *Comforter Cried* tears for you...while you were out misbehaving

But I never gave up on you, I cried tears like rain
Believing that all I invested in you was *Not In Vain*
You have acknowledged your sins and turned back to me
No matter how nasty, evil, sinful, dirty and *Filthy* you may be
I make this decree, *Let there be...*
Forgiveness, *Healing*, and restoration
Welcome home son, get ready for a great big *Victorious* celebration
Because at one time you were dead
But now that you have come home,
Truly, *We Have Some Brighter Days Ahead!*"

Living Water:

"*And he said, A certain man had two sons: And the younger of them said to his father, Father, give me the portion of goods that falleth to me. And he divided unto them his living. And not many days after the younger son gathered all together, and took his journey into a far country, and there wasted his substance with riotous living. And when he had spent all, there arose a mighty famine in that land; and he began to be in want. And he went and joined himself to a citizen of that country; and he sent him into his fields to feed swine. And he would fain have filled his belly with the husks that the swine did eat: and no man gave unto him. And when he came to himself, he said, How many hired servants of my father's have bread enough and to spare, and I perish with hunger! I will arise and go to my father, and will say unto him, Father, I have sinned against heaven, and before thee, And am no more worthy to be called thy son: make me as one of thy hired servants. And he arose, and came to his father. But when he was yet a great way off, his father saw him, and had compassion, and ran, and fell on his neck, and kissed him. And the son said unto him, Father, I have sinned against heaven, and in thy sight, and am no more worthy to be called thy son. But the father said to his servants, Bring forth the best robe, and put it on him; and put a ring on his hand, and shoes on his feet: And bring hither the fatted calf, and kill it; and let us eat, and be merry: For this my son was dead, and is alive again; he was lost, and is found. And they began to be merry.*" -Luke 15:11-24 KJV

"*If we confess our sins, he is faithful and just to forgive us our sins, and to cleanse us from all unrighteousness.*" -1 John 1:9 KJV

Poetic Insight:

Have you made a mess of your life? Have you made a mess of a particular situation? The problem with doing things our way is that our way doesn't always work. The prodigal son found himself in a strange land, estranged from his father and living beneath his privileges. He messed up. He was so low that pig slop was a meal option. He could have become comfortable and complacent in his sin and rebellion, but he didn't. He humbled himself and went to his Father and admitted his mistakes. His father received him, forgave him, and restored him! This poem tells the story of the Prodigal son, which speaks to God's willingness to receive us back when we've gone astray.

WALK OUT THE WORD:

Are you God's prodigal child? If so, return to him today. Read the story of the Prodigal son, Luke 15: 11-24, and ask for God's forgiveness. He is faithful and just to forgive you.

I am not ashamed of the gospel, because it is the power of God for the salvation of everyone who believes: first for the Jew, then for the Gentile. For in the gospel a righteousness from God is revealed, a righteousness that is by faith from first to last, just as it is written: "The righteous will live by faith.

Romans 1:16-18 NIV

FILTHY

I encountered someone today
And I don't think my life will ever be the same
I stood in shock as I heard the stranger whisper my name

Now, this guy was a sight to see
And I wondered, "How could he possibly know me?"
He smelled really bad and his clothes were dirty
He was absolutely filthy

His eyes were distant and cold
He had a young man's build,
But his face seemed very old

"Do I know you?" I asked Filthy
"Yes," He told me
We went to the same school, same church
Still, I didn't recognize him,
And Filthy's feelings were hurt

"I need your help," Filthy said
"How much do you need?," I asked with my wallet in hand
"No, no," Filthy said, "You don't understand,"
"I don't want your money, not one single dime"
"All I need is a few minutes of your time"

Filthy's story had been one of promise
A worshipper over the years
But something went wrong and here Filthy stood
Dirty, his eyes brimming with tears

He lived a lie, an image to portray
Felt pressured to perfection
In what he did and what he said
Was under constant scrutiny
He spoke of so called friends and family
Who didn't believe he could be
The Christian he claimed to be

Filthy, also told me
Of encounters with cold-hearted saints from the church and community
By now Filthy was shaking and his voice was weak
Though exhausted, he continued to speak
"Please friend, I need you to pray for me"

"I lost everything trying to portray an image that was never me
And now, I don't even know who I am supposed to be
I wander through life aimlessly,
Knowing mistakes and potential unfulfilled
Will be my only legacy"

With pain as extreme as his smell
This fellow had nearly been through hell
I saw a life once full of false accolades
I saw the need to be accepted still eating away
At the shell of this empty man
Who hoped one person would understand

He'd kept his pain to himself,
All his mistakes he tried to hide
No honesty with God, no friends to confide
He lost himself, who he was inside

Filthy looked at me and like a baby did he cry
Filthy handed me a tissue
I wiped his tears from my eyes
For if you look in the mirror long enough
You will meet the person behind the disguise

LIVING WATER:

"This is the message which we have heard from Him and declare to you, that God is light and in Him is no darkness at all. If we say that we have fellowship with Him, and walk in darkness, we lie and do not practice the truth. But if we walk in the light as He is in the light, we have fellowship with one another, and the blood of Jesus Christ His Son cleanses us from all sin.
If we say that we have no sin, we deceive ourselves, and the truth is not in us. If we confess our sins, He is faithful and just to forgive us our sins and to cleanse us from all unrighteousness. If we say that we have not sinned, we make Him a liar, and His word is not in us." -1 John 1:5-10 NKJV™

"For God so greatly loved and dearly prized the world that He [even] gave up His only begotten (unique) Son, so that whoever believes in (trusts in, clings to, relies on) Him shall not perish (come to destruction, be lost) but have eternal (everlasting) life. For God did not send the Son into the world in order to judge (to reject, to condemn, to pass sentence on) the world, but that the world might find salvation and be made safe and sound through Him.

He who believes in Him [who clings to, trusts in, relies on Him] is not judged [he who trusts in Him never comes up for judgment; for him there is no rejection, no condemnation--he incurs no damnation]; but he who does not believe (cleave to, rely on, trust in Him) is judged already [he has already been convicted and has already received his sentence] because he has not believed in and trusted in the name of the only begotten Son of God. [He is condemned for refusing to let his trust rest in Christ's name.]"
-John 3:16-18 AMP

Poem also refers to Luke 15:11-32 and Romans 10:9

POETIC INSIGHT:

This poem challenges us to be true to ourselves. So often as Christian believers we attempt perfection. We fail to remember that apart from God we can do no good thing and that even with our best efforts, our own righteousness is like filthy rags to God.

WALK OUT THE WORD:

If you could see yourself in this poem, it's time for an overhaul. Get alone with God and honestly share your heart and your hurts with him. He hears your prayer and He is able to heal you.

So then faith cometh by hearing, and hearing by the word of God.

Romans 10:17 KJV

QUESTIONS WORTH ASKING

Did I operate out of love,
Or did I just put on an act?
Were my actions motivated by concern,
Or knowing people would look for that?

Is my heart in the right place
Or I'm I just trying to save face?

Why do I do what I do?
To glorify God or make a name?
To please my Lord or you?

What are the underlying factors?
If all the world is truly a stage
Then am I just an actor?

Can I play my part, yet be real?
Do I judge and criticize,
Or do I to understand how others feel?

If your actions are right
But your attitude is wrong,
It's like your favorite singer lip-synching
While someone else performs the song.

LIVING WATER:

"If you love Me, keep My commandments." -John 14:15 NKJV™

"Though I speak with the tongues of men and of angels, but have not love, I have become sounding brass or a clanging cymbal. And though I have the gift of prophecy, and understand all mysteries and all knowledge, and though I have all faith, so that I could remove mountains, but have not love, I am nothing. And though I bestow all my goods to feed the poor, and though I give my body to be burned, but have not love, it profits me nothing. Love suffers long and is kind; love does not envy; love does not parade itself, is not puffed up; does not behave rudely, does not seek its own, is not provoked, thinks no evil; does not rejoice in iniquity, but rejoices in the truth; bears all things, believes all things, hopes all things, endures all things.

Love never fails. But whether there are prophecies, they will fail; whether there are tongues, they will cease; whether there is knowledge, it will vanish away. For we know in part and we prophesy in part. But when that which is perfect has come, then that which is in part will be done away. When I was a child, I spoke as a child, I understood as a child, I thought as a child; but when I became a man, I put away childish things. For now we see in a mirror, dimly, but then face to face. Now I know in part, but then I shall know just as I also am known. And now abide faith, hope, love, these three; but the greatest of these is love." -1 Corinthians 13:1-13 NKJV™

POETIC INSIGHT:

Why do you do what you do? Do you try to obey God and do the "right things" to prove your love for Him, or do you obey Him because you love Him. We can do all the "right things" and yet our hearts be far from God. It doesn't matter if you sing, preach, teach, pray, bake, cook, wash, visit, cut grass, usher, give money or send inspirational poems via e-mail. Your motive and the condition of your heart matters.

WALK OUT THE WORD:

Take some time to really look at your interactions with your family, friends, co-workers, church members, community groups, and your interactions with God Himself. Have a sincere "heart to heart" talk with God. Ask Him to show you where your thinking and motivations are not pleasing to Him. Repent where you have been wrong, ask God to create in you a clean heart (see Psalm 51) and turn your attention back to your relationship with Him.

FATHER, WHAT'S WRONG WITH DADDY?

(A collection of voices:)
Our Father which art in heaven, Hallowed be thy name
You are always present, always loving
But why are our Daddies on earth not the same?
(Voice #1)
It's not that my Daddy doesn't love me
The food on the table and clothes on my back shows just how much he cares
But in order to provide he is always working
It just doesn't seem fair
I would go without some CD's and outfits
If it meant he could spend more time here
(Voice #2)
Shoot, I can't really say that I feel for you
Because working is something my Pops seems determined not to do
He sleeps all day, and at night hangs out with his friends
Spending all of momma's hard earn ends
(Voice #3)
I never know what my Daddy is feeling or thinking
The only time he shows emotions is after he has been drinking
(Voice #4)
I never knew my Daddy at all
He left without looking back
No birthday gifts, no Christmas cards
Punk, could have at least called
(Voice #5)
My Daddy is spending his life in hell
He resides in a jail cell
Mother said that she fell
But "B****, I kill you"
Is what I heard him yell
I had to call the police, I had to tell
(Voice #6)
Life with my dad is like being in the reserves
Two weekends a month, and two weeks out of the year
The divorce has left me so disturbed
Daddy use to always be here
How could he leave me
He use to answer my questions
And calm my fears
(Voice #7)
My Daddy was never in the service

But he is really militant
I have to wash dishes a certain way,
I have to sit at the table a certain way
I have to do everything a certain way
HIS WAY
And if I don't do exactly what he say
Comments like "You are good for nothing"
Will precede the closed fist coming my way
(Voice #8)
I thought all the hell in my life stepped out
When my Daddy left, but then
My Step-Daddy stepped in
They look nothing alike
But act like evil twins
(Voice #10)
"AAAAAAAAAAAAAAAAAAAAAHHHHHHHHHHHHHHHHHHHHHHHH"
(Voice #11)
I knew it would take work
To get past the pain
So I went to my pastor
Because he was supposed to be
My Spiritual "Father" or "Daddy"
Alone in his office I told him all about the hurt
Session after session
I thought I was tripping when he appeared to flirt
But there was no mistake when he put his hands under my skirt
Because I resisted, I was kicked out the church
 (Voice #12)
My daddy has a secret identity
There's the good family man persona
He puts on for the whole world to see
And then there is his true identity
The cold hearted dictator
That's a secret to everyone
Except his immediate family
(A collection of voices:)
Father God, what is wrong with me
I know that I'm not supposed to be
But I'm jealous of people
Whose fathers are real daddies
Why me
My past has a tight hold
I try to move forward
But there are chains on my soul
Why me, God, why me
Can I ever be free?

(The voice of God)
The pain you feel is real
And I know most people don't understand
But you need to know
That I am not like man
Not only do I love you
I want to heal you
No, you did not bring this upon yourself
It was able to occur because of man's fallen state
I know you have considered giving in to the rage and hate
But for you, it is not too late
My children you can be free
If you open your hearts to me
(A collection of voices:)
Why should we trust you
Look at what you let us go through
(The voice of God)
Look at what I allowed Jesus to go through
(Selah)
Why did I allow Him to go through?
Because of my love for YOU
(Selah)
My children you can be free
If you open your hearts to me
You will see
That for you I can be
Both Father and Daddy

LIVING WATER:

When my father and my mother forsake me, Then the LORD will take care of me. -Psalms 27:10 NKJV™

POETIC INSIGHT:

No father is perfect. Some of us have great fathers. Some of us have no father at all. To fathers who are good and who are there for their kids, I thank you. You are not recognized enough.

But, some of us are laden with hurt and rejection concerning our fathers. You cannot move full steam ahead into your future, if you are being held in bondage by your past. Some of us have a hard time trusting God as our Father because we don't trust our fathers on earth.

When you can forgive your father, you will find peace and healing can begin.

Romans chapter 8 tells us that when we are Christ's and have the Holy Spirit we are adopted into God's family and we can cry Abba, Father. Abba is a term that shows great affection. God loves us so much that he let his only begotten son suffer so He could adopt us as His children.

WALK OUT THE WORD:

You may have experienced deep hurt at the hands of your earthly father, but begin to open your heart to God. He can be trusted. God can heal you, and your family.

Some fathers may never change. Seek to forgive them.

Ask God, our heavenly father to free you from your past so that you can experience the fullness of God's love and the fullness of your future. Go ahead, He is listening.

LOVE DOESN'T HIT

Closed fists, blackened eyes
Threats of "I will kill you"
Fear that you will die

But he says he loves you...

Tire iron and belt,
Pans and pots,
Seems you're getting hit with everything he's got

But he says he loves you...

Though you exchanged marriage vows
He forces you to have sex
"NO" still means "NO"
Your body he doesn't respect

But he says he loves you...

You can't finish school, not allowed to work
Masquerading as happy
On the occasional visits to church

But he says he loves you...

You're cut off from friends and family
Limited calls, and then he listens in
Checks the mileage on the car
To see where you've "really been"

But he says he loves you...

Police say, "It has to be three documented times"
Preacher says, "Stay and take it"
Mother says, "That's a good man"
Society says, "Keep quiet and fake it"

He says he loves you?

He says, "You caused this"
Then, "Baby, I won't do it again."
I say you deserve more than this
Love does many things, but love doesn't hit

Living Water:

"Let this mind be in you which was also in Christ Jesus, who, being in the form of God, did not consider it robbery to be equal with God, but made Himself of no reputation, taking the form of a bondservant, and coming in the likeness of men. And being found in appearance as a man, He humbled Himself and became obedient to the point of death, even the death of the cross." -Philippians 2:5-8 NKJV™

"Husbands, love your wives, just as Christ also loved the church and gave Himself for her," -Ephesians 5:25 NKJV™

"And you, fathers, do not provoke your children to wrath, but bring them up in the training and admonition of the Lord." -Ephesians 6:4 NKJV™

"Love suffers long and is kind; love does not envy; love does not parade itself, is not puffed up;" -1 Corinthians 13:4 NKJV™

Poetic Insight:

Love is about sacrifice. Love is the greater reaching down to the lesser and exalting the lesser higher than the greater. John 3:16a says, "For God so loved the world that He gave His only begotten son..." Jesus the Christ reached down to us and lifted us higher than himself. In other words, He put us before Him. He died for our sins so that we would not have to. The life of Jesus is love in action.

Walk Out The Word:

Domestic violence affects all races and socio-economic groups. This poem is geared toward women, but men are abused as well. No segment of society is immune. If you are being abused then please consider getting help. Do an Internet search for agencies and groups in your community that offer assistance. There are groups that help with counseling, shelter, and legal, financial, educational and career advice. Call the number below for help in finding local resources.

If you've never been in an abusive relationship, don't judge those who are in the midst of it. It is often a very complex situation and victims can't always see their way clear. Instead help that person by praying for their strength and directing them to persons/resources that will help them. If you are an abuser, please seek help today.

National Domestic Violence Hotline
24-hour, toll-free domestic violence hotline
1-800-799-SAFE

WARNING: If the topic of "Sexual Morality" is taboo for you than you may want to skip this week of FAITH Flow. My intentions are not to offend or stir debate but to look at the heart of the matter from what God has said. I pray that you will find this message to be beneficial to you and I hope you can appreciate the freedom that truth brings.

SOCIETY SAYS

Society says it's okay to have sex in the city
Society says that if you are a virgin than that is a pity
Society says you should do what feels right
Society says it's okay to take a stand, by lying down for one night
Society says if a wife is desperate, than she should cheat
Society says you are intolerant and closed minded
If you speak against people of the same gender sharing sheets
Society says play the field
Society says test out the goods before you commit
Society says say anything in order to hit and then split
Society says it's okay to explore
Whether you only cross certain boundaries fully clothed
Or if you are hardcore
Society says you got needs to fulfill
Society says nothing is wrong with a few thrills
Society says it's okay, if you two plan on getting married someday
Society says everybody is doing something
So don't let anything stand in your way
Society says that it's okay for me to compromise
As long as I sweeten some watered down gospel
And tell a few jokes to make you smile
Society says that it's okay to get with a
Weekend "friend" every once in a while
Society says men can go on the down low
And it's all good as long as their wives and girlfriends don't know
Society says it's okay for kids in the care of priests to be molested
Society says it's okay for sexual predators to go around unregistered
And not arrested because we have to make sure the predator's rights are protected
Society says that if you don't like the wife you got
Then you should consider a wife swap
Society says to a man that if she won't give it then he can take it
Society says that if you can't find anyone to give you the feeling you want
Then just buy a device that will make it
Society says that you can give your own self intimacy
Just send a donation to the billion dollar porn industry
Society says it's too hard to resist your urges, just give in and have fun

Society says AIDS will never happen to you
But look at history and learn from it
Remember the Trojan Horse had a secret threat and secret hole inside of it
Society says the Bible is just a guide
That we can pick and choose the parts we want to believe
Society says everything is relative
And truth can only be determined by how we individually perceive
Society says that what you decide is okay for you
Is exactly what you should do
As long as it doesn't infringe on anyone else
But that causes trouble that leaves hearts broke and minds stained
Because what one person does for sexual pleasure
Can and will cause another person pain
It could be physically, emotionally, spiritually, and/or mentally
Because unbridled lust focuses on self fulfillment
And even when between consenting adults often
Leaves the other person feeling ashamed and empty
This is not the way God our creator ordained things to be
God created sex to be enjoyed between a man and a woman
In the context of Holy Matrimony
And in that context only
God says our bodies are temples of The Holy Spirit
And that it's His will for us to avoid sexual immorality
God says He did not call us to be impure, but to live lives that are holy
Now it is okay if your opinion differs from the opinions expressed by me
However, God's word is truth and not opinion
So you see
When WE, disagree with what God says
Or when we say we agree but then act contrary
Or refuse to talk up for fear of controversy
Then with Society we agree
For it is from our misguided actions and silence
That strength is given to the voice of an immoral society

LIVING WATER:

"Do you not know that the unrighteous will not inherit the kingdom of God? Do not be deceived. Neither fornicators, nor idolaters, nor adulterers, nor homosexuals, nor sodomites, nor thieves, nor covetous, nor drunkards, nor revilers, nor extortioners will inherit the kingdom of God. And such were some of you. But you were washed, but you were sanctified, but you were justified in the name of the Lord Jesus and by the Spirit of our God."
-1 Corinthians 6:9-11 NKJV™

"For this is the will of God, your sanctification: that you should abstain from sexual immorality; that each of you should know how to possess his own vessel in sanctification and honor, not in passion of lust, like the Gentiles who do not know God; ...For God did not call us to uncleanness, but in holiness." –1Thessalonians 4:3-5, 7 NKJV™

"Flee sexual immorality. Every sin that a man does is outside the body, but he who commits sexual immorality sins against his own body. Or do you not know that your body is the temple of the Holy Spirit who is in you, whom you have from God, and you are not your own? For you were bought at a price; therefore glorify God in your body and in your spirit, which are God's." -1 Corinthians 6:18-20 NKJV™

"No temptation has overtaken you except such as is common to man; but God is faithful, who will not allow you to be tempted beyond what you are able, but with the temptation will also make the way of escape, that you may be able to bear it." -1 Corinthians 10:13 NKJV™

"I beseech you therefore, brethren, by the mercies of God, that you present your bodies a living sacrifice, holy, acceptable to God, which is your reasonable service. 2 And do not be conformed to this world, but be transformed by the renewing of your mind, that you may prove what is that good and acceptable and perfect will of God." -Romans 12:1-2 NKJV™

POETIC INSIGHT:

"Before we talk, let's get a few things straight...
1.) I am NOT perfect.
2.) I am NOT judging anyone.

"For all have sinned, and come short of the glory of God;" -Romans 3:23 KJV

"If we say that we have no sin, we deceive ourselves, and the truth is not in us. If we confess our sins, he is faithful and just to forgive us our sins, and to cleanse us from all unrighteousness." -1 John 1:8-9 KJV

But, the truth is that our bodies are the temples of the Holy Spirit. Sexual activity outside the context in which God ordained it (marriage between a man and a woman) defiles and damages our temples.

We have a lot of mixed messages where sex is concerned. We get messages from billboards, magazines, radio, TV, movies, books, and other people. There are people addicted to different sexual compulsions who feel hopeless. They may try to live like God has said but always seem to fail.

What God has said is what God has said. We have to hold His truth high above the dictates of society and high above personal desires. I am not judging you, but make no mistake – we all will be judged by the righteous Judge. I would like to point out that no one loves us more than God. God doesn't give us His commandments to make our lives difficult. God does not tempt us. God wants us to experience sex in a committed marriage where He has designed the act to be enjoyable and healthy. In that environment there is safety, trust and love.

If you are outside of God's will regarding your sexual lifestyle, repent. Repenting involves a turning away from sexual immorality and turning to God in a pursuit of purity. You may stumble, fall or give in to future temptations. f these things happen, sincerely ask God for forgiveness; get back up and keep moving forward in pursuit of purity.

Rejoice because we have been given truth and an opportunity to be forgiven. Remember that sin is sin. Sexual sins, gossiping, lying, stealing, murder and not forgiving are all viewed the same by God. We may not all have committed sexual sins, but we all have committed sin; there is no room for judgment.

Let's humble ourselves and pray. Let's seek God's face. Let's stand as a collective voice and say and do what God has said. That way what society says will be changed from a group of individual opinions that promote the pleasing of self, to one unified statement of truth that promotes God's word.

WALK OUT THE WORD:

Pray to God for an ever increasing passion to live in purity. Pray to God to reveal to you why purity is important to Him. Identify things that you should immediately stop doing that hinder purity. Set appropriate boundaries, and be mindful of your actions.

A VOW TO KEEP

I will take thee and thee only
To live together
In the holy state of matrimony
I will love and honor you
I will comfort and keep you
In sickness and in health
Whether rich or poor
We will always have wealth
The wealth of God's love
The wealth of our love
I will cherish every moment
Of this marriage ordained from above

LIVING WATER:

"Two are better than one, Because they have a good reward for their labor. For if they fall, one will lift up his companion. But woe to him who is alone when he falls, For he has no one to help him up. Again, if two lie down together, they will keep warm; But how can one be warm alone? Though one may be overpowered by another, two can withstand him. And a threefold cord is not quickly broken." - Ecclesiastes 4:9-12 NKJV™

"He who finds a wife finds a good thing, And obtains favor from the LORD." -Proverbs 18:22 NKJV™

"An excellent wife is the crown of her husband, But she who causes shame is like rottenness in his bones." -Proverbs 12:4 NKJV™

"Husbands, love your wives, just as Christ also loved the church and gave Himself for her, that He might sanctify and cleanse her with the washing of water by the word, that He might present her to Himself a glorious church, not having spot or wrinkle or any such thing, but that she should be holy and without blemish. So husbands ought to love their own wives as their own bodies; he who loves his wife loves himself. For no one ever hated his own flesh, but nourishes and cherishes it, just as the Lord does the church. For we are members of His body, of His flesh and of His bones. "For this reason a man shall leave his father and mother and be joined to his wife, and the two shall become one flesh." This is a great mystery, but I speak concerning Christ and the church. Nevertheless let each one of you in particular so love his own wife as himself, and let the wife see that she respects her husband." - Ephesians 5:25-33 NKJV™

POETIC INSIGHT:

The marriage vow is so very powerful. If you are married, take a moment to think back to the day you made your vow. Reflect on what your marriage vow means to you.

WALK OUT THE WORD:

Take a moment and look at the vows below. These are probably similar to the very vows that you took or will take on your wedding day. If you are married, reflect on the promise you made. I encourage husbands and wives to begin to recite these vows to each other often. Once a month, once a week, or daily keep these vows before you.

THE HUSBAND'S VOW:

Will you have this woman to be your wedded wife, to live together after God's ordinance in the holy state of matrimony? Will you love her, comfort her, honor and keep her in sickness and in health: and, forsaking all others, keep yourself only unto her, as long as you both shall live?

I _____take thee_____ to be my wedded wife, to have and to hold from this day forward, for better or for worse, for richer or for poorer, in sickness and in health, to love you and to cherish you, till death we do part, according to God's holy ordinance: and therefore I pledge to you my faithfulness.

THE WIFE'S VOW:

Will you have this man to be your wedded husband, to live together after God's ordinance in the holy state of matrimony? Will you love him, comfort him, honor and keep him in sickness and in health: and, forsaking all others, keep yourself only unto him, as long as you both shall live?

I _____take thee_____ to be my wedded husband, to have and to hold from this day forward, for better or for worse, for richer or for poorer, in sickness and in health, to love you and to cherish you, till death we do part, according to God's holy ordinance: and therefore I pledge to you my faithfulness.

RULES OF ENGAGEMENT

To win at all costs
Is to ensure your team a loss
Never go into an argument
With getting your point across
Being your only motivation
You may win the fight
But what's the cost of the devastation?

Left behind
You will find
That shooting from the hip
Causes unfounded accusations and hurtful declarations
To come from your lips

Things such as, "You always..." or "You never..."
Subtle and clever
How the enemy gets you two
To see each other as enemies
Instead of partners, lovers, friends, family and teammates
You should be seeking resolution
Not trying to show how great you can debate

Keep your voice down, there's no need to yell
Don't interrupt with "Whatever!", or "What the Hell?"
Let them finish before you speak...show some respect
Keep your emotions in check
Quit listening defensively
Which means stop anticipating
What you are going to say in defense
Or you could be left
Hearing only a piece of what your spouse had to say
And please leave yesterday in yesterday
Quit trying to make them pay
For what you say is already forgiven
Character is who they are... leave that alone
Talk about their specific actions... responsibility can be owned

Seek peace
Be willing to compromise
Not your integrity, but your point of view
Look at things from their eyes

How can two walk together

Unless they agree?
Proper conflict resolution
Is a key
To unlock the power and potential
In your marriage
Would you rather ride in a limo
Or travel by horse and carriage?

Effective communication skills
Can be learned if you are willing to try
You can use disagreements
To grow and laugh
Instead of divide and cry

If you want to make an argument
Work out for your good
First seek to understand,
Before seeking to be understood.

LIVING WATER:

"A soft answer turns away wrath, But a harsh word stirs up anger. The tongue of the wise uses knowledge rightly, But the mouth of fools pours forth foolishness. The eyes of the LORD are in every place, Keeping watch on the evil and the good." –Proverbs 15:1-3 NKJV™

"Finally, all of you be of one mind, having compassion for one another; love as brothers, be tenderhearted, be courteous; not returning evil for evil or reviling for reviling, but on the contrary blessing, knowing that you were called to this, that you may inherit a blessing. For

> *" He who would love life*
> *And see good days,*
> *Let him refrain his tongue from evil,*
> *And his lips from speaking deceit.*
> *Let him turn away from evil and do good;*
> *Let him seek peace and pursue it.*
> *For the eyes of the LORD are on the righteous,*
> *And His ears are open to their prayers;*
> *But the face of the LORD is against those who do evil."*

-1 Peter 3:8-12 NKJV™

"Let us therefore make every effort to do what leads to peace and to mutual edification." –Romans 14:19 NIV

"The tongue has the power of life and death, and those who love it will eat its fruit." -Proverbs 18:21 NIV

POETIC INSIGHT:

Disagreements will come, but disagreements don't have to bring disaster. There are "rules" that can help you and your spouse reach a productive solution. Look over the suggestions below.

1.) Seek first to understand where your spouse is coming from, then seek to be understood.
2.) Think before you speak.
3.) Don't be controlled by your emotions. You won't always be angry, but the effect of your words will always linger.
4.) Don't raise your voice. Use restraint and keep an even tone of voice. If you can't manage this amount of restraint, postpone the conversation until you can.
5.) Don't bring up things from the past that have already been resolved.
6.) Stick to the issues. Talk about the person's actions...not the person.
   (Don't use "you always" or "you never." Doing so attacks their character. Stick to the issues by   talking about specific actions of your spouse.)

7.) Be willing to admit when you are wrong and willing to ask for forgiveness. Understand that if
    there is conflict you may have contributed to it.
8.) Don't interrupt the other person while they are speaking. In the same regard, don't drag out your part of the conversation. State your viewpoint as clearly and concisely as you can.
9.) Don't listen defensively, meaning don't assume the position of someone under attack.
10.) Don't say or do anything just to "win", "make your point", or have the last "word".
11.) Honestly express how you feel. Try and understand your spouse's feelings and their logic as to why they feel the way they do.
12.) Seek a peaceful resolution. Pray for God's assistance and pray for God to give both of you clarity about the issue. Remember, you have help in the Holy Spirit. You don't have to figure this out on your own.

WALK OUT THE WORD:

Sit down with your spouse while things are calm and talk about these rules of fighting fair. These are tools that can be used to build a better relationship.

(BONUS FAITH FLOW ON MARRIAGE)

BECAUSE OF THREE

1 can only stand for so long
But 2 can help each other be strong
But what if 1 and 2 get weak on the journey
Thank God that THREE came from eternity
Because of THREE
This cord of unity can be held together
For the love and strength of 3
God, you, and me
Will last forever!!!

LIVING WATER:

"...A threefold cord is not quickly broken." -Ecclesiastes 4:12 NIV

POETIC INSIGHT:

Jesus is the essential part of your marriage. When a decision needs to be made in your marriage, the successful combination is not you, your spouse and your friend. It is not you, your spouse, and your parents. It is not you, your spouse, and your in-laws. It is not you and your spouse. The winning combination is you, your spouse, and Jesus.

WALK OUT THE WORD:

I encourage you and your spouse to take time at least once a week to pray together and study God's word together so that you can grow in your ability to hear Him as a couple.

INFIDELITY

This is based off the true story
Of someone you may/may not know
Read it carefully
Read it quickly/slow
There may/may not be clues as you go:
Their relationship was hotter than
Noon on the 4th of July
I'm talking 110 degrees in the shade
Not a single cloud in the sky
Sticky wet ice cream cones
Not able to stand being alone
Hand in hand through the park
Sneaking kisses after dark
Spark...ling conversation
Sweet anticipation
Of the next telephone call
Leave the puppy at home
This is true love yall
He/She was head over heels
Finally He/She said to their self
I know how real love feels
He/She stood at the alter
With their new Partner for life
He/She was overjoyed to become a Husband/Wife
Everything was great
As their commitment grew
They become known as the couple
Whose love always seem to be brand new
Where ever you saw one
Guaranteed to see two
They did thing everything together
They shared secrets, made decisions, gave each other strength
When He/She wasn't sure
Their Partner had the vision needed to go the length
Things begin to change ever so slowly
He/She was wholly...committed
But began to take their Partner for granted
Because He/She felt the relationship was firmly planted
He/She began to spend more time away
Leaving early, working late, or needing more time for personal play
Their Partner didn't say much
But notice that the amount of time began to increase
Between being touch

He/She began to converse less and less
He/She became more and more stress
He/She began to doubt their Partner
There was so many things the Partner had promise to do
But now He/She didn't have confidence that the Partner would come through
Decisions starting being made without everybody being involved
He/She started having struggles in which the Partner was not involved
He/She called an old Acquaintance
Wondering if the Acquaintance could help them solve
The struggles
The old Acquaintance said, "I will be there on the double"
The old Acquaintance came in dress to the nine
Smelling real good and looking fine
"I can't believe your Partner.
You would never go through this alone if you were mine!"
He/She knew that He/She shouldn't
Have call...after all
He/She had made a commitment to the Partner
But the Partner was not there
The old Acquaintance came quickly
And made it clear that feelings were still there
And if He/She was down
Then they could reconnect right here
He/She put their head on the Acquaintance's shoulder
Exhaled and began to cry
He/She told the Acquaintance all that He/She had been holding inside
He/She said, "I'm so scared, I don't know in life if I can win"
The old Acquaintance smiled through a sinister grin
Because doubt was the Acquaintance's way in
"You know the relationship with your Partner is one you should end!
Why trust and be committed to someone who is not true to you... when
You could just kick it every now and then
With a homey, lover/leech, friend"
He/She held the Acquaintance close
And whispered consent for the coming sin
"What are you doing?" came the question as the Partner walked in
I wonder how you think this story should end
But before you answer
Let me say that last part again...
Me/You held Fear close
And whispered consent for the coming sin
"What are you doing?" came the question as Faith walked in.
I hope you didn't miss the point
Of this story my friend
Just in case, I suggest you read it again
But this time when you go through

Here's what you do
Substitute He/She with YOU
Replace Partner with Faith
And put Fear where the word Acquaintance you see
Then answer this question honestly
Have you been true to your Faith
Or with Fear have you been committing infidelity?

LIVING WATER:

"For God did not give us a spirit of timidity (of cowardice, of craven and cringing and fawning fear), but [He has given us a spirit] of power and of love and of a calm and well-balanced mind and discipline and self-control." -2 Timothy 1:7 AMP

"There is no fear in love [dread does not exist], but full grown (complete, perfect) love turns fear out of doors and expels every trace of terror! For fear brings with it the thought of punishment, and [so] he who is afraid has not reached the full maturity of love [is not yet grown into love's complete perfection]." -1 John 4:18 AMP

"For all who are led by the Spirit of God are sons of God. For [the Spirit which] you have now received [is] not a spirit of slavery to put you once more in bondage to fear, but you have received the Spirit of adoption [the Spirit producing sonship] in [the bliss of] which we cry, Abba (Father)! Father!" -Romans 8:14-15 AMP

POETIC INSIGHT:

"Do you remember what it was like when you first believed? Do you remember having an unshakable faith in God? Do you remember what it was like to just spend time enjoying the goodness of God? Do you remember what it was like to be in love with Him?

Faith needs to be fed. Just like you have to grow and nurture any other relationship, you have to grow and nurture your faith. Have you found yourself doubting God lately? Are you having trouble believing just the basic elements of your faith? Do you constantly have thoughts that are rooted in fear? Are you making decisions based solely on your feelings?

If you are not diligent in maintaining your faith relationship, then you will provide an avenue for fear to creep in. Have you been opening up your most intimate thoughts and feelings to Faith or have you been being intimate with Fear? Sometimes keeping things right with Faith can be hard, but Faith is a committed partner who will bring hope, love, joy, and peace.

Fear on the other hand is just a one night stand that never uses protection because it wants to infect you with the deadly STD's (Spiritually Transmitted Diseases) of Terror, Doubt, Hate, Envy, Complacency, Selfishness, Depression, and Unbelief.

WALK OUT THE WORD:

End your illicit relationship with fear, repent of your infidelity, get tested and treated for any Spiritually Transmitted Diseases you may have acquired. Return to God, your first love.

WHEN YOU CALL HIM (The Name: Part II)

Please understand...

When you call on the name Jesus
Angels stand at command

When you call Him
All power is in His hand
You're not just calling a friend
He's not there just to bail you out again

He is the King
He is the King
He is the King
Of all Kings

Lamb of God
The Way, The Truth, and The Life
When you call on The Resurrection
Expect things to come back to life

Savior of the world
Not spiritual genie, nor cosmic bell-hop
Jesus is Lord of Lords
He's more than just a one-stop shop

JESUS, Alpha
JESUS, Omega
JESUS, Messiah
JESUS, Savior

JESUS, Redeemer
JESUS, Anchor
JESUS, Shepherd
JESUS, Master

Please understand...

When you call on the name Jesus
Angels stand at command

When you call Him
All power is in His hand
You're not just calling a friend

He's not there just to bail you out again

He is the King
He is the King
He is the King
Of all Kings

Lamb of God
The Way, The Truth, and The Life
When you call on The Resurrection
Expect things to come back to life

LIVING WATER:

"Wherefore God also hath highly exalted him, and given him a name which is above every name: That at the name of Jesus every knee should bow, of things in heaven, and things in earth, and things under the earth; And that every tongue should confess that Jesus Christ is Lord, to the glory of God the Father." -Philippians 2:9-11 NKJV™

POETIC INSIGHT:

We can't allow ourselves to become so familiar with Jesus that we forget who He is and what position He holds. Jesus is not only a friend, He is the King of Kings, He is the Lord of Lords, He is God Almighty. Let's not forget to honor Him for who He is.

WALK OUT THE WORD:

Study two characteristics of God. Look up the definitions of the words "Immutable" and "Sovereign". Then study the following scriptures, Hebrews 1:10-12 and Psalms 89:5-8. Call on Him with a fresh understanding that he is the Immutable Sovereign God.

FIRST THINGS FIRST

What should I make my priority?
Should it be money?
How about reputation and fame?
After all money answers all things
But great riches are worth less
Than a good name

Should I be my priority?
I'm just saying
When it is all said and done
Isn't life about looking out for number 1?

Hmm, sounds a little selfish
I do have a family
And doing what's in my wife's best interest
Cannot be making it all about me

How about my job
Or my ministry
Do I focus on keeping food on the table?
Or do concentrate on helping others become free

I will put family above it all
That seems honorable and noble
Or, did I just make an idol?
Is providing the best for my family
The will of God, or did
I just make family God's rival?

Career, Family, Food, Clothes
All these things are needed
But all cannot be number one

What's the single most important thing to get done?

Here's the answer according to God's only begotten son

We find in Matthew 6:33 Jesus tells
"Seek first the Kingdom of God and His righteousness
And all these things will be given to you as well."

Kingdom is God's government
The way He expects things to run

Righteousness is being in right relationship with Him
Step one, is being in right relationship with His Son

Accepting Jesus is just the beginning
Christ is the door
Don't just stand at the entrance
Step in and see what the Kingdom has in store

Make sure you make it top priority
To remain in right standing
By growing in intimacy
With Father, Holy Spirit, and Son
It will then be easier to understand
How God has decreed things should be done

LIVING WATER:

"Therefore I tell you, do not worry about your life, what you will eat or drink; or about your body, what you will wear. Is not life more important than food, and the body more important than clothes? Look at the birds of the air; they do not sow or reap or store away in barns, and yet your heavenly Father feeds them. Are you not much more valuable than they? Who of you by worrying can add a single hour to his life? But seek first his kingdom and his righteousness, and all these things will be given to you as well. Therefore do not worry about tomorrow, for tomorrow will worry about itself. Each day has enough trouble of its own." - Matthew 6:25-27, 33-34 NIV (emphasis mine)

POETIC INSIGHT:

Our time is precious. When we don't prioritize we end up wasting time. We can also put off doing the most important things while going after things that don't mean as much. We should invest our time in learning about God's kingdom and developing a right relationship with God. When we do that the other things we often put in front of God will be added to our lives.

WALK OUT THE WORD:

Do an inventory of the time you have spent this week. How much time did you spend working? How much time did you spend eating? How much time did you spend relaxing? How much time did you spend with family? How much time did you spend with friends? How much time did you spend developing your relationship with God and learning about God's kingdom? Conducting a time inventory will give you an idea of what you prioritize.

CHILDLIKE FAITH

With simple trusting eyes they look up
Motioning with their hands for you to pick them up
Expecting you to refill their Sippy cup

They run and play
Never having a thought of how they will eat that day
They trust you to understand
Even when you can't interpret what they are trying to say

They have no fear
They cry when in need
They are not too prideful to shed a tear

They simply believe
They simply trust
And we have to be like them
We simply must

LIVING WATER:

"And they brought young children to him, that he should touch them: and his disciples rebuked those that brought them. But when Jesus saw it, he was much displeased, and said unto them, Suffer the little children to come unto me, and forbid them not: for of such is the kingdom of God. Verily I say unto you, Whosoever shall not receive the kingdom of God as a little child, he shall not enter therein." –Mark 10:13-15 KJV

POETIC INSIGHT:

This poem seeks to remind us of what it means to simply trust our powerful and loving God to take care of us.

WALK OUT THE WORD:

Do you still believe God can do anything? If not, seek to re-establish your child-like faith.

God, who has called you into fellowship with his Son Jesus Christ our Lord, is faithful.

1 Corinthians 1:9 NIV

CITIZEN

I'm in this world
But not of it
I'm a Kingdom citizen
And I love it
I operate
According to divine government
Patience instead of hurry
Prayer instead of worry
Must be bold
No time for scary
Blessed and highly favored
Love my neighbor
Pray for those who hate me
Give and it shall be given
Principles of royal living
No time for retreating
I'm a Kingdom citizen

LIVING WATER:

"But Paul said to them, "They have beaten us openly, uncondemned Romans, and have thrown us into prison. And now do they put us out secretly? No indeed! Let them come themselves and get us out." And the officers told these words to the magistrates, and they were afraid when they heard that they were Romans. Then they came and pleaded with them and brought them out, and asked them to depart from the city."
–Acts 16:37-39 NKJV™

"I do not pray that You should take them out of the world, but that You should keep them from the evil one. They are not of the world, just as I am not of the world. Sanctify them by Your truth. Your word is truth."
-John 17:15-17 NKJV™

POETIC INSIGHT:

The dictionary defines "citizen" as a native or naturalized member of a state or nation who owes allegiance to its government and is entitled to its protection.

If you accept Jesus Christ as your Lord and Savior than you are "Born Again" into the Kingdom of God. As a citizen of the Kingdom of God you have certain rights and are entitled to protection. The Kingdom of God is God's government.

WALK OUT THE WORD:

If you want to learn more about what it means to be a kingdom citizen, might I suggest a book on the topic of the kingdom by Dr. Myles Munroe.

AMBASSADOR

I represent the Kingdom of God
As an ambassador
I'm on official government business
When I come through the door

Homes and businesses
Throughout the neighborhood
My mission: To infiltrate and dominate
With the news that is good

That's gospel, not gossip
Truth about the Holy One
That's God, there is only one
He sacrificed His only begotten son

I have authority
Which equals RIGHT
My words have power
Which equals MIGHT

If I speak opinions
Tainted by sight
Though commissioned to speak
My words will not be right

So I speak only
What my King has spoken
I'm to stay in prayer
So communication is never broken

I have a home country
This world is only where I operate
To the world's culture I can't conform
I must not assimilate

I herald the coming of the Kingdom
But I also bring the Kingdom when I come
So as it is in Heaven
God's will on Earth be done

Living Water:

"And Jesus came and spoke to them, saying, "All authority has been given to Me in heaven and on earth. Go therefore and make disciples of all the nations, baptizing them in the name of the Father and of the Son and of the Holy Spirit, teaching them to observe all things that I have commanded you; and lo, I am with you always, even to the end of the age. Amen."
-Matthew 28:18-20 NKJV™

Poetic Insight:

We are all charged to be ambassadors for Christ. Live a life that reflects his goodness.

Walk Out The Word:

Find ways to communicate the love of Jesus without speaking a word. Our actions are the clearest indication of what is in our hearts.

STAND

It has stood for nearly
1500 years

The earth shook and trembled
But, it stood

The waters came
It withstood the flood

Others felled,
Rot,
Chopped,
Burn,
Cut,
But, it stood

Land was exchanged
Slaves were brought

Wars were fought
But, it stood

It stood through the hurricane
Lives lost, homes destroyed
Government sending envoys
Power is out
School is closed
Over a decade later
Damage is still seen from the storm of a lifetime
It took some blows, but it stood

Once it could fit inside an infant's palm
But now it can hold grown men

It is a majestic, magnificent
Awe inspiring
Testament
To the truth of Psalms 1:3

Rooted and grounded
Flourishing in its season

I stood, looking up at a tree

that stands over ten times taller than me
Wondering, "If God did this from an acorn,
What all can He pull out of me?"

LIVING WATER:

Blessed is the man Who walks not in the counsel of the ungodly, Nor stands in the path of sinners, Nor sits in the seat of the scornful; But his delight is in the law of the LORD, And in His law he meditates day and night. He shall be like a tree Planted by the rivers of water, That brings forth its fruit in its season, Whose leaf also shall not wither; And whatever he does shall prosper. The ungodly are not so, But are like the chaff which the wind drives away. Therefore the ungodly shall not stand in the judgment, Nor sinners in the congregation of the righteous. For the LORD knows the way of the righteous, But the way of the ungodly shall perish.
-Psalm 1:1-6 NKJV™

POETIC INSIGHT:

The Angel Oak is a massive and majestic oak tree on Johns Island, SC. This tree, with its huge trunk and massive limbs, is an estimated 1400-1500 years old. I was moved as I realized that something that was once an acorn grew into this beautiful tree.

In Psalm 1 we have a description of the righteous person who meditates in God's word both day and night. That person will be like a tree planted by the rivers of water. They will bring forth their leaf in their season. When I look at this tree and see God's work, I am humbled and inspired. As magnificent of a sight the Angel Oak is above ground I would really like to see what it is like underground. Its root system must be massive and must tap into sources of water that are far beneath the earth's surface.

This is yet another reminder. Our spiritual root systems need nourishment, even if drought abounds all around. Remain rooted and grounded in the word of God to maintain your balance.

WALK OUT THE WORD:

Read and meditate on Psalm 1. Pay special attention to the actions of a blessed person. Position yourself for greatness by taking delight in God's word.

OPEN ACCESS

I was rejected
Now walls have been erected
Heart is password protected
Afraid to let anyone close
Don't want anyone to see
Shame, guilt, lust, filthy
Struggling with me
So I veil myself
I hide in plain sight
Small talk, so my pain isn't obvious
What?
You want to get close to me?
You can't without a special coded key
Please enter your password
What's the last four of your social?
Mother's maiden name?
High school mascot?
Model of your first car?
God,
I want to let you in
I hear you calling out to me
But can you guarantee
That if I let you see
The real me
That you won't send me to hell immediately?

(The voice of God):
I know that you were hurt, I was too
I know that you were rejected, I was too
I was hurt and rejected by you
After being hurt and rejected for you
I know about your past
I know about your lies
I know about your pain
I know about your mistakes
I know about your sin
I took the penalties and pain
So that you can live life free
From guilt, fear, shame, hurt,
I was held so that you could live in liberty
I was rejected so that you could
Live life with joy and victory

With me, you can win
With me, new life can begin
I just need you to let me in

LIVING WATER:

"So, as the Holy Spirit says: "Today, if you hear his voice, do not harden your hearts..." -Hebrews 3:7-8 NIV

"For God so loved the world that He gave His only begotten Son, that whoever believes in Him should not perish but have everlasting life." -John 3:16 NKJV™

POETIC INSIGHT:

In today's society we have to protect everything. We are almost to the point of having passwords for our passwords.

It is possible to go through life just brushing the surface. We can have full conversations about weather, sports, politics, and even God without ever really showing others who we are.

God is calling out to us. When we don't allow Him in we are also keeping ourselves from entering into His presence. By denying Him access to us, we also deny ourselves access to Him.

WALK OUT THE WORD:

Let God in today. It is safe to show Him who you really are. He can be trusted with your information. His P.I.N. is John 3:16 and his privacy policy can be found in 1John 1:8-10, and Isaiah 43:25.

DADDY'S GARDEN
(Dedicated with love to my father, Peter S. Smith Sr.)

You're late!
I said sarcastically to the sun
Who do you think you are,
Coming up an hour after the work has begun?

I looked around
I was surrounded by plants and dirt
No such thing as summer vacation
In Dorchester, there was summer work

Daddy had me in the fields at the age of five
Back then I thought that he was the most unfair person alive

I had to dig holes, plant seeds
Water the plants, chop down the weeds

I'm not talking about a little garden
I'm talking a farming industry
Machines were invented to do what I was doing
But no, daddy was old school
He didn't want a machine to ruin his produce
So I felt he produced me...

Bean picker, peanut picker, corn gatherer
Okra cutter, pea sheller, potato planter

I hated working in the field and the sun hated me
He would take his hottest beams and shine them right down on me

This does not make any sense; they have grocery stores for a reason

Finally, we would go home, but the work didn't end
The sun laughs and then goes to sleep
But not us
Daddy hangs a huge light on the side of the barn
We have to wash what we've gathered
Separate what we are going to sell from what we are going to keep

Some were sold, some were eaten, some were canned, some were frozen
Others were left to produce seed for the next year,
Many were given

What a strange experience for a child
People laughed at us
Family, friend, and foe alike
You know, it's funny
They always wanted something from us
Not willing to come to the fields to help get the crops out
But when hunger kicked in they stood with their hands out

I couldn't wait to escape, I had to get free
When I'm grown, no more fields for me

But then I grew up

And strangely enough
God started teaching me His plan
Concepts and principles
About the Kingdom and about being a man

Seed time and harvest. Delayed gratification.
Sowing and reaping. Giving produces gain.
Being joyful regardless of life's weather,
Because there is a need for both sunshine and rain

Don't eat your seed, plant it and watch it multiply
Protect your investment, keep a watchful eye
Choose the right soil, rotate your crops
You can always gather harvest
As long as your sowing never stops

Be careful who you let help
But help all who you can

God, I understand

It's the lessons of my childhood
Being taught all over again
The things I thought I would never need
Are the very things I have to know to win

Now I am grateful for the work ethic
And knowledge that my daddy sowed into me

I left my daddy's fields
Only to find myself in my Heavenly Father's vineyard
His yoke is easy and His burden is light
But there have been times where the days were long and hard

However, this time the Son shines down on me
Not to be cruel, but to restore and replenish me

It's amazing
As a youngster, I thought when I got older
And looked back on working in the fields
That I would be mad and that my heart would be hardened
But now that I am a man
I thank God for the love I received
And the lessons I learned in my Daddy's Garden

LIVING WATER:

"While the earth remains, Seedtime and harvest, Cold and heat, winter and summer, And day and night Shall not cease." -Genesis 8:22 NKJV™

"Do not be deceived, God is not mocked; for whatever a man sows, that he will also reap." -Galatians 6:7 NKJV™

POETIC INSIGHT:

I learned invaluable lessons growing up in the country and working in the fields. The principle of seed time and harvest was instituted by God during creation and it will remain as long as the earth does. You cannot plant corn and expect to receive a harvest of green beans. It will not happen. If it does, you'd better not eat them!

As a man sows so shall he reap. This principle applies to more than just vegetables. It applies to everything in life. Each day is new, but nothing in your life will be new if everything about you is old. If you want this to be a better year, then you are going to have to sow better seeds. You cannot meet your weight loss goal by sowing large amounts of fatty foods as regular parts of your diet. You cannot get out of debt by sowing the same spending habits that got you into debt.

When my father wants a crop of potatoes, he plants potatoes. When he wants peanuts he plants peanuts. You will have to sow for what you want and for where you want to go. The first thing is to sow the word of God into your heart for as a man thinks in his heart so is he. (Proverbs 23:7) What you believe will affect what you think, what you think will affect what you do, and what you do will affect who you become.

You will also have to take practical actions to sow and protect your seeds. I am not talking about name it and claim it, and I am not talking about if you think about it long enough it will eventually happen. What I am talking about is work. Believing is essential and tremendous power is released by making confessions and declarations. You have to do these spiritual things but you also have to do natural things and that means going through a process. I had to go out in the field and dig holes to put the seeds in. I had to make sure the holes were deep enough. The ground you choose is very important. Sometimes I had to water the seed. Listen, carrying heavy buckets of water on a hot day is not easy, but it was necessary for the each plant's survival.

I would later have to come back to the field with a garden hoe to chop down weeds that grew up around the plant. The weeds would overtake the plants and field if nothing was done to prevent it. Sometimes the weeds would come back, which meant having to repeat the process. You have to take measures to protect what you are sowing for and working towards. I am talking months of work and process to bring about what was sowed for.

When the harvest came there was more work. We had to go out and gather immediately. If left in the field too long the harvest could rot. The animals would return to feast on the crops. Worst of all, the people who laughed at us would come and steal crops when they thought we would not be around. Beware, there are people staying close enough to you so that they will be able to steal your harvest after you have done all the work.

After getting the crop, then came the decision of what to do with it. Some of it we ate and enjoyed. However, most of it was used to cause increase. This was done in three ways. First, some of the crop was always given (sowed) into people. Then most of the crop was sold. And last, some of the crop was kept to be used as seeds to produce the next year's harvest. Don't eat all of your harvest.

WALK OUT THE WORD:

Re-invest some of what you have gained. Apply this to your own life. This could mean investing financially, investing your time, investing your talents, etc.

THE DENESHIA DECREE

Born of woman, in a month known to be cold
Came forth such a passionate soul
The very fingers of God formed her frame
Deneshia, the baby girl was named
Because of her birth
Earth, could never be the same
For she was destined with divine purpose
Even before she came
But as she grew she encountered an enemy
An enemy who told her she was ordinary
He said she was ugly and destined for poverty
He said she was not strong enough to endure
At one time she used to be so sure
Of her God and of her call
She had such overwhelming joy when she forsook all
To follow her Lord
Now the enemy's lies have cut like a sword
Into her very essence
Making it hard to feel God's presence
Her confidence and strength are like sea waves that are tossed
Demons hide in shadows whispering all hope is lost
She prays and presses forward
Determined to stand
For her foundation is solid rock, not that loose sand
Deneshia is determined to hold to her Master's hand
Even though exhaustion and fatigue stalk her throughout the land
The enemy sends frustration, confusion, and stress
Their mission: Get Deneshia to believe the lies, make her life a mess
Through her travels she meets a king
Whom she encourages tremendously
In return he makes a royal proclamation
The following is the Deneshia Decree...

No rubies could possibly match your wealth
For you are one of the rarest treasures on earth
A woman who can be described as virtuous
Deneshia you are eternally victorious
No one will be able to stand against you all the days
Of your life, for God is with you as He was with Moses
Through God your days will be many
And to the years of your life He will add length
Your clothing is honor and strength
Righteousness is your breastplate

The belt of truth grips your waist
Daily the word of God you embrace
Causing the renewal of your mind, which is encased
In salvation
Your feet have received preparation
To take the peace of the gospel to the nations
For through you it's been declared all nations shall be blessed
You are Abraham's seed
The covenant God established with him, is established with you indeed
Your roots run deeper than riverfront oak trees
You are firmly planted
Never will you be like the chaff
Which is carried away by the breeze
The wicked, even your enemies and foes
Who shall come to eat up your flesh
Have already stumbled and fell
Nothing shall by any means hurt you
For you have power to tread on serpents and scorpions
And over every enemy from Hell
You are more majestic than snow capped mountains
Able to nurture and bring forth life
Like living water coming from an ebony fountain
Among the daughters your love is as
The lily among thorns
Your presence brings warmth and hope
Deneshia's arrival is the dawn... of a spring morning
At your voice joy leaps in the hearts of men
To hear you speak is to hear the bluebird sing
From within you echo the sounds of wisdom
Your arms house understanding
Mothers thank God for your impact on their children
Because into those young ladies
You sow your virtuous heart
Living proof that if you teach them the ways of righteousness
When they are old, from this path they shall not depart
You are humble enough to be exalted
Ever yielding, so that the Master Potter can continually mold
Your good name and loving favor is chosen rather than silver and gold
Beautiful does you no justice
Because the image you portray is not your own
For you are made in the image and likeness
Of the living God who can never be dethroned
You have no choice but to rule and reign
Dominion is your destiny
Dominate in all things and give Jehovah the glory
For you are not your own
But she who was brought with a price

The very blood of Jesus Christ
Who thought it not robbery to become our sacrifice
You are seated in heavenly places
Angels are encamped all around
Any thoughts exalting themselves against the knowledge of Christ
Are immediately cast down
There are so many jewels in your crown
Your heart is in heaven, because that is where your treasure lies
Seeking first the Kingdom is your top priority
And according to His riches in glory by Christ Jesus
All your needs our Father shall supply
You live every day with such energy, zest, and zeal
For it is settled in your heart and mind
That by the stripes of Jesus the Christ you are healed
You keep wise counsel, you move in humility
But make no mistake
Your words could crush armies
A thousand shall fall at thy side, and ten thousand at thy right hand
But it shall not come nigh thee
For you dwell in the secret place of the most high
Abiding under the shadow of the almighty
Where you learn to divide the word of truth rightfully
Sweet is thy fruit
Love, joy, peace, longsuffering, gentleness, goodness, and faith
Are all things the Holy Spirit produces in ye
Along with meekness and temperance
Because of this no law can stand against thee
You rejoice not in iniquity, but rejoice in truth
And though you may not have your own
Book like Esther or Ruth
When your final mission is complete
And from this place you have gone
Throughout the ends of the earth you will be known
As one of the greatest
Among daughters, sisters, aunts, wives, lovers, and friends
Deneshia, you are God's leading lady
Who shall overcome the world
And receive your promise of a victorious end
For God decreed your success
Even before time had a chance to begin

LIVING WATER:

"He who finds a wife finds what is good and receives favor from the LORD."
-Proverbs 18:22 NIV

"Who can find a virtuous wife? For her worth is far above rubies. The heart of her husband safely trusts her; So he will have no lack of gain. She does him good and not evil All the days of her life. She seeks wool and flax, And willingly works with her hands. She is like the merchant ships, She brings her food from afar. She also rises while it is yet night, And provides food for her household,
And a portion for her maidservants. She considers a field and buys it; From her profits she plants a vineyard. She girds herself with strength, And strengthens her arms. She perceives that her merchandise is good, And her lamp does not go out by night. She stretches out her hands to the distaff, And her hand holds the spindle. She extends her hand to the poor, Yes, she reaches out her hands to the needy. She is not afraid of snow for her household, For all her household is clothed with scarlet. She makes tapestry for herself; Her clothing is fine linen and purple. Her husband is known in the gates, When he sits among the elders of the land. She makes linen garments and sells them,
And supplies sashes for the merchants. Strength and honor are her clothing; She shall rejoice in time to come. She opens her mouth with wisdom, And on her tongue is the law of kindness. She watches over the ways of her household, And does not eat the bread of idleness. Her children rise up and call her blessed; Her husband also, and he praises her: " Many daughters have done well, But you excel them all." Charm is deceitful and beauty is passing, But a woman who fears the LORD, she shall be praised. Give her of the fruit of her hands, And let her own works praise her in the gates." -Proverbs 31:10-31 NIV

POETIC INSIGHT:

This poem is dedicated to my wife and best friend, Deneshia.

WALK OUT THE WORD:

If you are unmarried, ask God to direct you to his best choice for you in a spouse. You will not be disappointed!

FLOW AGAIN

Focus, Love, Overcome, Win ... FLOW Again
Can't see the forest for the trees?
Go Paul Bunyan
Until nothing stands to block the breeze

Fix your eyes forward, keep your head straight
Success is close, no longer a long wait
Patience has done her part
Beware... Distraction, is the guardian of the gate

Focus
Love
Overcome
Win
FLOW Again

Love lifted me; old school, it's my favorite hymn
Present day truth so powerful it's a gem
It is love that lifted me, not me that lifted me
Pride is a Deceiver, Humility is the mark of a Believer

Love all unconditionally
According to the description in 1 Corinthians 13
Love all passionately
Those who dirty your name, are ones you ask God to forgive and clean

Focus
Love
Overcome
Win
FLOW Again

More than a CONQUEROR
Victory is my starting line
Fight is finish before is starts
Because the battle isn't mine

No weapon formed can prosper
Against you Hell may bombard
Keep the faith; God is the fence of your defense
Evil will not get through

Focus
Love
Overcome
Win
FLOW Again

Rejoice in His joy
Sing of God's strength
Grace and Mercy
Gave you the boost you needed to go the length

Today you are a champion
Doesn't matter how messed up yesterday might have been
Every day that you are breathing
Is a day that you win

Focus
Love
Overcome
Win
FLOW Again

LIVING WATER:

"Let your gentleness be evident to all. The Lord is near. Do not be anxious about anything, but in everything, by prayer and petition, with thanksgiving, present your requests to God. And the peace of God, which transcends all understanding, will guard your hearts and your minds in Christ Jesus."
-Philippians 4:5-7 NIV

"And so faith, hope, love abide [faith--conviction and belief respecting man's relation to God and divine things; hope--joyful and confident expectation of eternal salvation; love--true affection for God and man, growing out of God's love for and in us], these three; but the greatest of these is love." -1 Corinthians 13:13 AMP

"What, then, shall we say in response to this? If God is for us, who can be against us? He who did not spare his own Son, but gave him up for us all— how will he not also, along with him, graciously give us all things? Who will bring any charge against those whom God has chosen? It is God who justifies. Who is he that condemns? Christ Jesus, who died—more than that, who was raised to life—is at the right hand of God and is also interceding for us. Who shall separate us from the love of Christ? Shall trouble or hardship or persecution or famine or nakedness or danger or sword? As it is written: "For your sake we face death all day long; we are

considered as sheep to be slaughtered. "No, in all these things we are more than conquerors through him who loved us. For I am convinced that neither death nor life, neither angels nor demons, neither the present nor the future, nor any powers, neither height nor depth, nor anything else in all creation, will be able to separate us from the love of God that is in Christ Jesus our Lord." -Romans 8:31-39 NIV

POETIC INSIGHT:

Do you feel stuck in a rut? Turn your attention to your love relationship with Christ. What happen to the passionate intimate worship you use to experience with Him? Make time to better your relationship with Him. Return to the basics. Pray, read the Bible, and take some quiet time to spend with the Lord. No amount of choir practice, preaching, teaching, or witnessing can replace your time spent in personal fellowship with God.

WALK OUT THE WORD:

What is your flow? What rivers (talents, gifts) did He place inside of you? If you don't know, ask God to reveal them. Then let those gifts flow in a way that glorifies God.

For we walk by faith, not by sight.

2 Corinthians 5:7 NKJV™

BELIEVE AGAIN

What happens to a dream deferred?

Does it shrivel up and die?

Naw,

Grapes of promise may be gone

But even they leave evidence of hope

By becoming raisins when they dry

Tis not over, nowhere close

Pick up the pen again,

Start up your business again,

Open your heart again,

Trust Jesus again,

Run the race to win,

Believe again!

LIVING WATER:

"Jesus said to him, "If you can believe, all things are possible to him who believes." -Mark 9:23 NKJV

POETIC INSIGHT:

Don't be afraid to succeed. It doesn't matter how much pain, mistakes, or failures are in your past. Trust God again, try again and believe again. Your destiny awaits!

WALK OUT THE WORD:

It's simple. Believe again!

For it is by grace you have been saved, through faith—and this not from yourselves, it is the gift of God— [9]not by works, so that no one can boast.

Ephesians 2:8-9 NIV

ACCORDING TO YOUR FAITH

Vision impressed upon their souls
You have one chance

To be whole

Go beyond what you can see

With eyes malfunctioning

Visualize what is yet to be

Defining moments

Can't be defined

By circumstance

Purposed, not chanced

Blind one, take a glance

Into what is to be

See beyond sight

Faith beyond fright

Go to other side

No matter how bumpy the ride

See, believe,

Believe, See

Faith

Evidence

Word

Guarantee

Future

Your choice

Do you believe what you have been shown?

Or do you believe what you see?

LIVING WATER:

*"As Jesus went on from there, two blind men followed him, calling out,
"Have mercy on us, Son of David!"*

When he had gone indoors, the blind men came to him, and he asked them, "Do you believe that I am able to do this?" "Yes, Lord," they replied. Then he touched their eyes and said, "According to your faith will it be done to you"; and their sight was restored..." -Matthew 9:27-30a NIV

POETIC INSIGHT:

This poem was written from Cape Town, South Africa. I went to an AIDS hospital to encourage the patients. I left inspired and encouraged by a woman named Elizabeth. Her African name being Funiwe. She spoke with such faith, conviction, joy, and peace. She possessed great faith! She said, "You come back next year and I won't be in this place. I believe that I will be healed." She wasn't talking about being healed because she would be in heaven, she was talking about being at her home in South Africa with her son. She had a vision of what she believed God for. Just like the blind men in the scripture, she possessed an inner vision that is greater than her circumstances. I did not return to South Africa the following year and I don't know the exact outcome of her situation. But, I'm confident that her faith was not disappointed.

WALK OUT THE WORD:

Close your eyes to your surroundings and situations. With your eyes shut allow your inner vision to show you what can and will be.

SLEEP AND EAT

I was running on E
Empty
Now I'm running on fumes
The future looms
With reports of doom and gloom
I'm trying to keep up
Trying to push through
Smiling and saying I'm blessed
When I feel like I'm through
What to do?

Working harder and harder
With no pay increase
Don't know if the budget shortfall
Will cause my job to cease
People jumping on my last nerve
Feel like taking a swing
But I continue to serve
Feeling stressed, depressed, blue
What to do?

Going in circles
Not going very fast
Enemy's whispering
That I won't last
Now I'm being tested
Will I pass?
Or give in to sin
Only to repeat the class
What to do?

 "...If anybody asks you
What's the matter with me..."
Tell them
I'm frustrated, aggravated
Tired and hungry
Looking for deep revelation

Something super spiritual
But first get your affairs in order
God isn't into empty rituals

What to do...

Take a look at the prophet,
And what God had Elijah do
Sleep and then eat
Have a helping of soul food
So I slept and ate
Knelt to tell God my problems
And get some things off my chest
But I decided to praise Him
And tell Him why He's the best

I fix another plate –
Wait...
The headache has left the room
I feel joy
Boy...oh...boy
And I will not be moved
Feeling strength again
My perspective is changing
Starting to believe I can win

I needed to slow down
Long enough to refuel
Clear my mind, find my peace
Keep my cool
Let this be an example for you
If you're on the brink of defeat,
We should overflow, not run low
Take time to sleep and eat

LIVING WATER:

"Now Ahab told Jezebel everything Elijah had done and how he had killed all the prophets with the sword. So Jezebel sent a messenger to Elijah to say, "May the gods deal with me, be it ever so severely, if by this time tomorrow I do not make your life like that of one of them." Elijah was afraid and ran for his life. When he came to Beersheba in Judah, he left his servant there, while he himself went a day's journey into the desert. He came to a broom tree, sat down under it and prayed that he might die. "I have had enough, LORD," he said. "Take my life; I am no better than my ancestors." Then he lay down under the tree and fell asleep. All at once an angel touched him and said, "Get up and eat." He looked around, and there by his head was a cake of bread baked over hot coals, and a jar of water. He ate and drank and then lay down again. The angel of the LORD came back a second time and touched him and said, "Get up and eat, for the journey is too much for you." So he got up and ate and drank. Strengthened by that food, he traveled forty days and forty nights until he reached Horeb, the mountain of God." -1 Kings 19:1-8 NIV

POETIC INSIGHT:

In 1Kings 18 Elijah was used by God to orchestrate one of the greatest miracles recorded in the Bible. In 1Kings 19 (right after the miracles of chapter 18) Elijah is scared and running for his life. Elijah goes into the desert and prays to die. He says that he has had enough. How could he go from one of the greatest moments of ministry to being suicidal?

After the elated feeling from the miracle began to pass Elijah felt tired and alone. He believed that he was the only prophet of God left. He was physically tired and emotionally drained. Have you ever been there? Have you ever been exhausted? Do you currently feel like giving up and giving in? Do you feel guilty about feeling that way because you can obviously see that God is with you? Are you having great success at work, in school, in ministry but feel like a wreck on the inside? Is the world celebrating your success while your family hurts with a private pain?

Elijah fell asleep and God sent him some food to eat. Elijah slept and ate and was able to journey for forty days. Sometimes we have to push our way through, but we must also realize that there are times when we are not supposed to push. We need to make it a point to take care of the basics. We are not designed to work through lunch every day. We are not designed to work year round and never take vacation. We are not designed to operate off of four hours of sleep. We are not designed to minister to every family accept our own. We are not designed to worry. Stressed and depressed should not be our default setting.

Take time to eat today and enjoy the meal. Turn your phone off. Take a walk or sit in a park (or anywhere you can have peace and quiet) and pray. Tell God how wonderful He is to you. Tonight, don't allow the pressures of the day or worries about tomorrow to be the thoughts you drift off to sleep with. Make it your goal to pray and think on peaceful things before going to sleep.

While in South Africa I learned some words in Afrikaans. Afrikaans is one of the official languages of South Africa. The word baie means thank you and dankie means very much. It means "Thank You Very Much." This poem is my personal thanks to God.

BAIE DANKIE

God,
Baie Dankie for my life
For strength and health
The active use of my limbs
And for riches and wealth

You've blessed me with a sound mind
And a good education
I have peace that surpasses all understanding
Baie Dankie for my Salvation

I am grateful for my career
As well as a willingness to work
Grateful for gifts and talents
And for how you heal hurts

Baie Dankie for my friends
Baie Dankie for my family
Baie Dankie for my prosperous businesses
Baie Dankie for ministry

Lord,
I appreciate the food I eat
Also, the clothes I wear
I give you praise for the roof over my head
And because you are always there

You've blessed me so...
My wonderful relationship
New transportation
Debt cancellation
And credit restoration

Baie Dankie for family reconciliation
Baie Dankie that I can wash myself and clothe myself too
Baie Dankie that I can read the Bible in peace
Baie Dankie for the privilege of praying to You

I don't take for granted
That I can see, smell, hear and talk
Baie Dankie that I can feel and taste
I am grateful for the ability to walk

What would I do without your grace and mercy
Your complete forgiveness and unfailing love
I praise you for warm days filled with sunshine
And for cold days when rain falls from above

Baie Dankie for being so patient with me
Baie Dankie for blessing me abundantly
Baie Lord, Baie Lord, Baie Dankie

So often I question, murmur, cry and complain
Showing little gratitude
And the gratitude I express is often rushed, with little thought and sincerity
Baie Dankie Lord for revealing my hypocrisy to me
And Baie for another opportunity
To say that for all who You are and for all that You do
Lord, I love you and I sincerely thank you.

Living Water:

"Now on his way to Jerusalem, Jesus traveled along the border between Samaria and Galilee. As he was going into a village, ten men who had leprosy met him. They stood at a distance and called out in a loud voice, "Jesus, Master, have pity on us!" When he saw them, he said, "Go, show yourselves to the priests." And as they went, they were cleansed. One of them, when he saw he was healed, came back, praising God in a loud voice. He threw himself at Jesus' feet and thanked him--and he was a Samaritan. Jesus asked, "Were not all ten cleansed? Where are the other nine? Was no one found to return and give praise to God except this foreigner?" Then he said to him, "Rise and go; your faith has made you well." -Luke 17:11-19 NIV

"O give thanks unto the LORD; call upon his name: make known his deeds among the people." -Psalms 105:1 KJV

Poetic Insight:
We always have something to be thankful for. To give thanks is a command. To obey is a choice.

Walk Out The Word:
Give thanks with a grateful heart!

ECONOMIC STIMULUS

(Voice 1)
Milk or medicine
Gas or lights
How should one fight
This plight

Stimulate the economy
Send aid
Check was spent two months in advance
Back to waiting to get paid

There has to be a better way

It already rained,
So now I need to put some away
For a bright, sunny day

Trying to decide whom to pay
Robbing Peter to pay Paul
Dodging phone calls

I know...Righteous people should pay their bills
And do it on time
Lord you multiplied fish and bread
What can you do with this last dime?

(Voice 2)
God can stimulate your economy like no other
It rained down bread when Israel needed to be fed
They went from slave to free and wealthy
In just one night
You can see today
Because years ago God said let there be light
His word is true and it cannot return to Him void
It will accomplish its task
Can He do anything with your dime you ask?

Son, what has been written? What has been promised?

(Voice 1)
"But remember the LORD your God, for it is he who gives you the ability to produce wealth, and so confirms his covenant, which he swore to your forefathers, as it is today."   -Deuteronomy 8:18 NIV

Lord, it's not that I don't remember
But choosing between power and food
Is difficult in the cold of winter

Why should I give to the church?
When preacher seems to be living fat
And when I go for help
I can't get any of my donations back

"Bring ye all the tithes into the storehouse, that there may be meat in mine house, and prove me now herewith, saith the LORD of hosts, if I will not open you the windows of heaven, and pour you out a blessing, that there shall not be room enough to receive it. And I will rebuke the devourer for your sakes, and he shall not destroy the fruits of your ground; neither shall your vine cast her fruit before the time in the field, saith the LORD of hosts. And all nations shall call you blessed: for ye shall be a delightsome land, saith the LORD of hosts." -Malachi 3:10-12 KJV

Those expecting payment for car and insurance
Don't give a care how much I sing blessed assurance

"Let everything that has breath praise the LORD. Praise the LORD."
-Psalm 150:6 NIV

How do I praise when things are so tight
I love you sincerely, but I get harassed at night
"Ring, Ring"...Lord, I know I owe, but that's not right

"Let no debt remain outstanding, except the continuing debt to love one another, for he who loves his fellowman has fulfilled the law."
-Romans 13:8 NIV

(Voice 2)
I remember being where you are

I remember facing possible eviction, no place to stay
I remember trusting God to make a way
I remember getting my own place and not having to pay

I remember the car being taken
I remember faith being shaken
I remember catching rides to work
I remember the pain, disappointment, hurt

I remember having four jobs at the same time
I remember going to three on the same day

I remember waking up unemployed
I remember not having any pay on the way

I remember getting a new ride that was very old
Oil leak, gas leak, window broken, cold
I remember the times that try a person's soul
I remember side of the road
Car broke, hitch hiking with hope
No lunatic would offer a lift

I remember the gift
New vehicle, here is the key
I remember crying because someone
Did this for me

Being broke is not holy,
Don't fall for that story
But being content is necessary
Even as you be confident
That there is more in store...
Don't forgot to thank Him
Even if your home is a dirt floor

"I know what it is to be in need, and I know what it is to have plenty. I have
learned the secret of being content in any and every situation, whether well
fed or hungry, whether living in plenty or in want."
-Philippians 4:12 NIV

He has a way of doing everything He promised
When you feel like doubting, remember what he told Thomas

"Then Jesus told him, "Because you have seen me, you have believed;
blessed are those who have not seen and yet have believed."
-John 20:29 NIV

You don't need money as much as you need a new mentality
God wants you to have the best and the best is He
Look first to His face
Understand who He is, not just what He can do
He loves you
He has given you mercy, love, forgiveness, and grace
You have first place
When it comes to His affections
You belong to His kingdom
Which means you and your finances have a right to kingdom protection
But first you need to be in right standing
Seek first His kingdom and His righteousness

Enter into His gates with thanksgiving
Recognize that you are already blessed
Enter into His courts with praise
For what you are expecting Him to do
Pray back to Him what He has already said to you
Study His word on finances and put into practice what He has said to do

Give God at least ten percent
But don't get reckless with the other ninety
Be faithful over little
Until He blesses you with plenty
Wealth includes family, friends, love and health
You may not have a dollar but have extreme wealth
Our entire focus cannot be money
When we hear prosperity
However, He never intended for you
To have a poverty mentality
Your hope is not in the lottery

Be diligent and do your work unto the Lord
Honoring Him in all that you do
Give cheerfully and His blessings
Without sorrow, will cause increase to you

Save, Invest, Lend
Not spend, borrow and spend

Let me say that again...

Save, Invest, Lend
Not spend, borrow and spend

This is not the first time you have been challenged
This is not the last time He will come through

Stay calm; be led by faith not fear
Do what you need to do
Cut back, take a class, budget
Be humble and ask someone who knows more than you
And make sure you are letting the good news (the gospel)
Be the news you speak and the news you allow to speak to you
Say what God has said about your financial state
And remember that He is never late

Living Water:

"Which of you by taking thought can add one cubit unto his stature? And why take ye thought for raiment? Consider the lilies of the field, how they grow; they toil not, neither do they spin: And yet I say unto you, That even Solomon in all his glory was not arrayed like one of these. Wherefore, if God so clothe the grass of the field, which today is, and tomorrow is cast into the oven, shall he not much more clothe you, O ye of little faith? Therefore take no thought, saying, What shall we eat? or, What shall we drink? or, Wherewithal shall we be clothed? (For after all these things do the Gentiles seek:) for your heavenly Father knoweth that ye have need of all these things. But seek ye first the kingdom of God, and his righteousness; and all these things shall be added unto you. Take therefore no thought for the morrow: for the morrow shall take thought for the things of itself. Sufficient unto the day is the evil thereof."
-Matthew 6:27-34 KJV

"Beloved, I wish above all things that thou mayest prosper and be in health, even as thy soul prospereth." -3 John 1:2 KJV

"Where there is no vision [no redemptive revelation of God], the people perish; but he who keeps the law [of God, which includes that of man]– blessed (happy, fortunate, and enviable) is he." –Proverbs 29:18 AMP
"So also faith, if it does not have works (deeds and actions of obedience to back it up), by itself is destitute of power (inoperative, dead)."
–James 2:17 AMP

Poetic Insight:

Headlines may relay words of fear and chaos across the global financial markets. There may be bleak outlooks – budget cuts and layoffs – in various places. Things may not look good and may sound even worse.

I am not a financial counselor. I simply want to remind you to trust God more than ever during these times. Study what the Bible says about finances and find practical things that you can do to better your financial situation. Continue to pray for His insight and leading.

Walk Out The Word:

Look up, study, and apply the following scriptures to your financial life:

Matthew 25:14-28

Luke 19:11-26

Luke 16:1-14

Proverbs 13:22

1Timothy 5:17-18

Philippians 4:10-19

Proverbs 11:24-25

2 Corinthians 9:6-11

Matthew 6:20-21

Luke 6:38

Proverbs 19:20

Proverbs 12:15

1Timothy 5:8

Proverbs 30:25

Also, I encourage you to visit www.crown.org to find financial tools, education, and insight that you can apply to your family finances.

WHERE THERE ARE TEARS

(*Voice of God*)
People are hurting and they need to see Me
So I am sending you
Hearken to their cry
Lift your hands so that I can dry their eyes

Don't know your purpose
Look for the tears
If you have a solution
Your purpose is there

Where there are tears
That's where you need to be
What you do for the least
You actually do for Me

(*Voice of FLITE*)
Thirst is stealing life away
You can provide water today
In the street bodies lay
Kneel and pray

Lives shattered
Homes destroyed
Mass confusion
Soldiers deployed

Death is circulating
Fear is escalating
Does anyone care
About the tears?

Pray for stability
Pray for hope
Pray for safety
Pray they can cope

All knees on deck
This is not a drill
It could have been you
Whose family was killed

Compassion is needed
Leave criticism at the door
Pray against aftershocks
This disaster doesn't need an encore

Where mothers cry
For children who cannot respond
Where children have become orphans
And love ones are buried with no coffins

Where there are tears
That's where you need to be
Christ says what you do for the least
You do for Me

LIVING WATER:

"When the Son of Man comes in his glory, and all the angels with him, he will sit on his throne in heavenly glory. All the nations will be gathered before him, and he will separate the people one from another as a shepherd separates the sheep from the goats. He will put the sheep on his right and the goats on his left.

"Then the King will say to those on his right, 'Come, you who are blessed by my Father; take your inheritance, the kingdom prepared for you since the creation of the world. For I was hungry and you gave me something to eat, I was thirsty and you gave me something to drink, I was a stranger and you invited me in, I needed clothes and you clothed me, I was sick and you looked after me, I was in prison and you came to visit me.'
"Then the righteous will answer him, 'Lord, when did we see you hungry and feed you, or thirsty and give you something to drink? When did we see you a stranger and invite you in, or needing clothes and clothe you? When did we see you sick or in prison and go to visit you?'

"The King will reply, 'I tell you the truth, whatever you did for one of the least of these brothers of mine, you did for me.'
"Then he will say to those on his left, 'Depart from me, you who are cursed, into the eternal fire prepared for the devil and his angels. For I was hungry and you gave me nothing to eat, I was thirsty and you gave me nothing to drink, I was a stranger and you did not invite me in, I needed clothes and you did not clothe me, I was sick and in prison and you did not look after me.'

"They also will answer, 'Lord, when did we see you hungry or thirsty or a stranger or needing clothes or sick or in prison, and did not help you?'
"He will reply, 'I tell you the truth, whatever you did not do for one of the least of these, you did not do for me.'

"Then they will go away to eternal punishment, but the righteous to eternal life." -Matthew 25:31-46 NIV

POETIC INSIGHT:

Tears often indicate pain. When people are in pain, there is an opportunity to show the love of God. If you have an answer to a person's pain then you have found purpose. God will use our hands, our words, our hugs, our prayers, our dollars, our skills, and everything else we are willing to let Him use. Are you searching for your calling? Whose tears bring you to tears?

On January 12, 2010, a major earthquake caused catastrophic damage to the county of Haiti. Many lives were lost. This flow was written as a call to action to help the people of Haiti. The recovery effort will take years. Let's do everything we can to help our neighbors.

WALK OUT THE WORD:

Take time to pray for those in need. Take time to give to those in need. Whether the need is that of a country or an individual, we should make it a point to help others in their time of need.

In addition to all this, take up the shield of faith, with which you can extinguish all the flaming arrows of the evil one.

Ephesians 6:16 NIV

THE PROMISE

Has anyone ever made you a promise they didn't keep
Have you ever went back on your word
Causing another person to lose sleep
Has anyone ever told you everything would be okay?
But they looked even more scared than you
Have you received that phone call?
That leaves you crying and wondering what in the world you're going to do?

Have you experienced getting tragic news out of the blue?
Have you ever thought a situation was bad,
Only to find out it was worse than anticipated?
Ever wondered why the evening news isn't "R" rated?
Are the bill collectors calling more than your own family?
Or do you wish it was a bill collector when you see
Certain relatives on the caller I.D.?

Does your past make you unsure of your present?
Are you constantly wishing to go back to days that were good?
Is crime taking over your neighborhood?
Is your mind always running at full speed?
Do you miss the moment,
Because you are thinking about what you need to do
Tomorrow, next week or what you should have done yesterday
Is worry your drug of the day?

Will "Too Busy" be the only words your obituary needs to say?
Without your calendar will your life be thrown into total disarray?
Do your thoughts breed fear?
Are you nervous around everyone,
And even more nervous when no one is there?

Are you tired, fatigued, drained?
Does the thought of your life causes you pain?
Do you secretly fear your life will not get any better?
Have you ever thought about penning a suicide letter?

Are you feeling overwhelm and on edge?
Do people use you and make you feel like you don't matter?
Are conversations with family and friends filled with empty chatter?
Are you tired of being underrated?
No matter how hard you try, is it never appreciated?

Is your job leaving you frantic and stressed?
Is your home, your office, your car, your mind, your life
A mess?
If your answer to any of these is yes
Please know there is hope, so take a deep breath, and prepare to be
Blessed...

(Intermission: Take a deep breath. I am serious. Breathe in, breathe out, breathe in, breathe out. Clear your mind for a moment, and open your heart. Now hug yourself. Seriously, hug yourself. Wrap your arms across the front of you until your hands are on your shoulders and give yourself a gentle squeeze. Tell yourself that God loves you, and then tell yourself that you love you. See, that wasn't so bad was it? Stop wondering what your co-worker will think, you know you don't like them anyway. You have been through a lot and still have some more to go through but your life is not over, and it will get better. If you want to know how, then let's go back to the poem.)

...You can trade in your life of worry, fear, fatigue, and stress
For a life full of peace, hope, joy, and rest
Jesus made us a promise
That He would not leave us comfortless
And the promises of Jesus are the best
Because His promises never fail, no matter what the test

For Jesus himself is our peace
And he destroyed the barrier,
The dividing wall that was keeping God and us apart
So let the peace of Christ rule in your hearts

Don't be anxious about anything
Because through Christ who strengthens you
You can do all things
A heart at peace gives life to the body
You can lie down and sleep in peace
Knowing that God alone makes you dwell in safety

Perfect love casts out fear
Guard your heart with all diligence
And don't let any seeds of terror and doubt be planted there
Remember, God really does love you and holds you dear

No matter who broke their promise, lied, disappointed or deceived you
God can be trusted; the promises of Jesus are always true
Life can get rough, but no matter what you are going through
Your life may not get easier but it can be better
If this one thing you will always do

Believe, receive, and hold on to
The peace of God that surpasses all understanding
That has been made available to you

LIVING WATER:

"These things have I spoken unto you, being yet present with you. But the Comforter, which is the Holy Ghost, whom the Father will send in my name, he shall teach you all things, and bring all things to your remembrance, whatsoever I have said unto you. Peace I leave with you, my peace I give unto you: not as the world giveth, give I unto you. Let not your heart be troubled, neither let it be afraid." -John 14:25-27 KJV

"And the same day, when the even was come, he saith unto them, Let us pass over unto the other side. And when they had sent away the multitude, they took him even as he was in the ship. And there were also with him other little ships. And there arose a great storm of wind, and the waves beat into the ship, so that it was now full. And he was in the hinder part of the ship, asleep on a pillow: and they awake him, and say unto him, Master, carest thou not that we perish? And he arose, and rebuked the wind, and said unto the sea, Peace, be still. And the wind ceased, and there was a great calm. And he said unto them, Why are ye so fearful? How is it that ye have no faith? And they feared exceedingly, and said one to another, What manner of man is this, that even the wind and the sea obey him?" -Mark: 4:35-39 KJV

POETIC INSIGHT:

I saw a true story about three friends who went up for a ride in a small airplane. Only one of the three knew how to fly. Shortly after takeoff the pilot had a heart attack and died. Not only do the other two guys have to deal with the fact that they just watched their friend die, they don't know how to fly the plane. They couldn't work the radio and thereby couldn't call for help. But they managed to fly the plane. They flew around the tower at the airport trying to signal that they were in trouble then they crash landed barely missing an apartment building. By the grace of God they both survived.

Has something unexpected happened that has left you scrambling or bewildered? Do your family and friends sense that something is wrong and are trying to reach out to you? Listen, try to work the radio. Try to communicate. The first distress call should be made to God. He can step right into the plane, get in the pilot's seat (not co-pilot) and fly you to your original destination or bring you down with a safe landing.

Perhaps you cannot point to a single incident that has thrown your life off course. But a series of events have left you with minimal peace. Are you too busy for your family and friends? Are you to busy for God? (Side note: Doing God's work and spending time with God is not the same thing!) Are you too busy for yourself? Are your thoughts full of fear, dread, worry, and stress? Are you living or are you just existing?

In the scriptures above we see the disciples and Jesus on a boat. Jesus is down below sleeping and the disciples are up above encountering a storm. As the wind arose and the waves beat the ship the disciples got scared and went below to wake up Jesus asking if he cared that they perish.

The first thing we need to note is that Jesus told them to go to the other side. If He says go to the other side, then you will make it to the other side. What happens between here and the other side cannot stop you unless you allow it to.

The second thing is that Jesus is down below asleep. If the ship would have starting sinking, then Jesus would have been the first one the water would have gotten to. Jesus is in the most dangerous location and He is sleeping peacefully. Are you going through some rough storms in your life and God doesn't seem concerned? God isn't worried. God may be silent at the moment just to see if you will speak up. Jesus woke up and spoke to the wind and sea, saying, "Peace, be still." How about you? Will you take a stand today and begin to speak to the storms in your life?

WALK OUT THE WORD:

If you want the peace of God that has been made available to you, remember what Philippians 4:6-7 has instructed us to do:

"Be careful for nothing; but in everything by prayer and supplication with thanksgiving let your requests be made known unto God. And the peace of God, which passeth all understanding, shall keep your hearts and minds through Christ Jesus."

MERCY, MERCY ME

I stood facing the judge
Trying to speak on my own behalf
My words were muffled
The prosecutor laughed
Slowly I took my seat
My lawyer smiled confidently
But I smelled defeat
The prosecutor stood
It was his turn
He whispered, *"My closing arguments*
Will make sure that you burn"
He wasted no time
Replaying the details of an imperfect life
The life that is mine
He accused me of many things
His argument was eloquent and articulate
My character, my integrity, my reputation
All took major hits
He twisted many things
And distorted many facts
Told outright lies
And brought in "witnesses" to confirm them
I was indeed worthy of the death sentence he sought
"Your Honor, the battle of faith
He claims hard to have fought
But what about the questionable stuff he brought
And those bad things he thought
Oh, not to mention the places he went
I got him on camera to back up that
If that's not enough then surely
You can't ignore that some of his dark actions were outright FILTHY

With that the prosecutor rested his case
He sat with a smirk of certain victory on his face
Then something unexpected took place
A rather large insect crawled out to the middle of the floor
It asked, *"Your Honor, may I approach?"*
The prosecutor yelled, *"A talking insect!"*
"Approach," the judge spoke
"Your Honor I have information pertinent to this case,"
Said the insect
The judge motioned to the witness stand
The insect crawled up to the top of the stand and

Begin to testify
"Your Honor what I have to say is true and not a lie
I don't know if this fella did the things of which he is accused
He might be as guilty as sin
But I hope his freedom he wins
Your Honor some years ago, soon to be ten
I was crawling around in a place
Where arguably I should not have been
I was in the defendant's office space
He saw me and a look of disgust came on his face
I felt the wind as his shoe went up in the air
I knew my life was over
I knew he was going to crush me right there
But he paused
I shuddered in terror as he hesitated
I braced myself for the death blow
But he put his foot down, just stared and waited
Then I was suddenly lifted into the air
A sheet of paper
Became a makeshift elevator
He walked me down the hall, out the door
And down the steps
My little insect heart leapt
With joy as the paper touched the ground
I crawled off it and scampered to safety
Your Honor, he did not have to
But the defendant went out of his way to save me!"
The judge looked at the insect
He looked at the prosecutor
Then at my lawyer, and finally at me
He said, "You may not be innocent
But because of your mercy
I show you mercy
I pronounce you not guilty
You may go free"

Living Water:

"Blessed are the merciful: for they shall obtain mercy."
- Matthew 5:7

Poetic Insight:

Grace is when we get what we don't deserve. Mercy is when we don't get what we do deserve. I learned a valuable lesson several years ago. I was doing an internship and one day at the office I saw a huge insect going across the floor. My first instinct was to kill it. As I got up to do so I felt God telling me not to kill it. "It's just a small bug," I responded. "What do you think you look like in my sight?" was God's reply. I was stunned! God was not saying that He looks on us with disgust like I would an insect. He wanted me to understand that just like the bug, I was small and powerless compared to His power and might. Though it was an unusual example, I was being taught a lesson on mercy. I got a sheet of paper, scooped the bug onto it, took it outside and let it go. I had mercy on one of God's smallest creatures. Now, I have killed insects since that day; living in the south, I'm sure I will kill them again. But, I never forget that lesson and I try to space as many critters as possible.

Since that day at the office I have found myself in situations where I really needed mercy. I can't help but wonder about the grief and hurt I avoided by my obedience to God that day in the office when he taught me about mercy.

For some of you, it may be too strange to show mercy to bugs. That's understandable. Start with humans and work your way down (smile).

You will encounter someone who needs your mercy. They may have used all their days off but still need to miss a day of work; they may need to be hired despite their criminal record; they may need someone to listen, though they are not a good listener; they may need help getting out of a mess that they got themselves into. Pray about each situation, get God's guidance and be willing to extend the level of mercy as He instructs. You're not meant to respond to every need. But always remember that blessed are the merciful: for they shall obtain mercy. The life you end up helping, changing or saving could turn out to be your very own.

Note: You can obtain eternal mercy and forgiveness of your sins by accepting Jesus Christ as your personal Lord and Savior. When you stand before God, if you are saved by Jesus Christ, you will be deemed innocent of sin though your life was never perfect. Jesus has paid death's penalty on your behalf.
If you have never given your life to Jesus by accepting Him as your personal Lord and Savior, then please consider receiving Christ today. There is information how to accept Jesus Christ as your personal Lord and Savior on pages 153 and 154.

WALK OUT THE WORD:

Show someone mercy today. Offer goodwill to someone who, due to their actions, may not deserve it.

STABILITY

Life may move like an ocean's wave
Life may jolt like a road unpaved
People may change in an instant
Finances may grow from great to infant
What appears sure today
Can be gone tomorrow
Feasting on loaves of worry
And a bowl of sorrow
The words, "I don't know"
Echo
As uncertainty grips your heart
And your life appears to fall apart
Half empty is your cup
Hope & Faith appear to have given up
However, God is steadfast
His word is sure to last
God is not moved by circumstance
He doesn't lead by chance
He is sure, He is confident
He is pure, He is consistent
God is still able
God is stable

LIVING WATER:

"God is our refuge and strength, an ever-present help in trouble. Therefore we will not fear, though the earth give way and the mountains fall into the heart of the sea, though its waters roar and foam and the mountains quake with their surging." -Psalm 46:1-3 NIV

"Heaven and earth will pass away, but my words will never pass away." -Luke 21:33 NIV

POETIC INSIGHT:

God is steadfast. God is consistent. God is trustworthy. God is not afraid. God is not worried. When the things and people in your life seem unsure, you can rest assured that God is still God.

When you sit down in a chair you are communicating that you have faith in that chair's ability to support you. However, if you saw that a leg on the chair was loose, then you would hesitate before sitting on it. You might even try to steady it with your own hand before putting your full weight on it.

If your life seems like that wobbly chair or if you already fell off of the chair of life, the thought of depending on someone or something to fully support you may make you feel resistant or anxious. Still, I urge you to take a seat in God's presence and relax in His ability to hold you. Take your hands off the situation. God is steadfast. God is balanced. God is faithful. God is stable. He doesn't need you to steady the chair.

WALK OUT THE WORD:

Look up what God has said about your situation. You can use the commentary in the back of your Bible, get a book on God's promises, or use the internet. One resource I would recommend is www.biblegateway.com . You can type health, finances, etc. into the search box and it will bring up scriptures pertaining to that word. Pick one or two scriptures and think about them all day. When you have to say anything about your situation make sure your comments correspond with God's word.

EITHER

Either He is who He says He is or He isn't
God is either all powerful or has no power at all
Either all knowing or has no clue
God is either loving or doesn't give a crap about me and you

Either He is provider or He isn't
Either He is protector or He isn't

Either He is faithful or none of it is true
Either He is almighty or lacking the might needed to come through

He is Omnipotent
He is Omniscient
He is Immutable
He is Sovereign

He is who He says he is
Or
He isn't

He said all things are possible with Him
He said He would never leave me nor forsake me
Either He will or He won't
Either I believe or I don't

LIVING WATER:

*"For the Son of God, Jesus Christ, who was preached among you by me
and Silas and Timothy, was not "Yes" and "No," but in him it has always
been "Yes." For no matter how many promises God has made, they are
"Yes" in Christ. And so through him the "Amen" is spoken by us to the glory
of God. Now it is God who makes both us and you stand firm in Christ. He
anointed us, set his seal of ownership on us, and put his Spirit in our
hearts as a deposit, guaranteeing what is to come."*
-2 Corinthians 1:19-22 NIV

POETIC INSIGHT:
Worry comes when there are areas that we don't fully trust God in. We can
waste an incredible amount of time and energy worrying about things we
cannot control.

WALK OUT THE WORD:

Trust God. He's trustworthy.

ACKNOWLEDGEMENTS

I would like to thank God the Father, God the Son, God the Holy Spirit. Lord Jesus, without you, this would not be possible. I pray that you are pleased.

Deneshia, thank you for the many hours you have invested into *Faith Flow*. I am so blessed to be able to call you my wife.

Thank you to Peter S. Smith Sr., (the hardest working retiree I know), Margaret Smith (the greatest mother the world has known), David V. Graham (the chess champion), Loretta Surgeon Graham (you express love in so many ways), Katrina, Peter Jr., and Genobia (I love y'all. You have no idea how proud I am of each of you), Evonne; Mary, Bernard and Vanessa and their spouses (the coolest in-laws), Derrick "D-Law"(Keep doing what you doing), Javonne (published at the age of 13, WOW, use your every gift for God's glory), Peter III, Marquis, Kenyatta Jr., Shantel, Miles (Your futures are amazingly bright), To the entire Smith, West, Graham, Surgeon and Maybank Family, I love you all.

R.I.P.: Eartha Mae Smith (Nana), Eugene Smith (Uncle Ceifus), Thomas Ezell (Uncle Mack), Jessie C. West (Granny), Vernon Cummings (Cousin "V.C."), Antonio J. Cannon, Jr. (Lil' Tony).

Spiritual Covering: Redemption World Outreach Center, Apostles Ron and Hope Carpenter, Redemption Ministerial Fellowship International, Dr. Paul and Karyl Gaehring (The blessing from the head is truly flowing down)

Many Thanks to: Sharon Datcher (I am humble and honored by the way you featured my works on your site); Pastor Tony Snipes (www.ArtLessonsFromGod.com) – You're a wonderful mentor; Kenyatta Pooser Sr. (We got the phat party going on, down here on…E.T.P.!); Sista Sepia (www.sistasepia.com) - Thank you for inspiring me and for all of your support; Chris & Nacole Paetz, James & Erica Goldsmith, Jeremy Goldsmith, Mr. George & Apostle Annie Broughton, Pastor Benjamin & Mrs. Vernice Williams, Freedom Worship and Praise Center, Rev. H.J. Mack, Dr. & Mrs. Curtis Hill, The ministry of Bishop Eddie L. Long, Pastor & Mrs. Rodney Bolden, Rev. Zebra Pinckney, Anthony Kelly, Lona Dunston, Joy Smith, Altheia Richardson, Almeda Jacks, Starlett Craig, Gail Johnson, Dr. Brad Jones, Pastor M.F. Jackson, Larry Lother, Pastor Greg Smith, the men of M2M, Pastor Hasker Hudgens, Mike & Jennifer Parker, Mike Darnell, Operation GO!, Teen Impact, Brenda Woods, Redemption Marketplace Academy, Julian & Shante' Nixon, Stan & Sherrica Sims, Jahmal & Vanessa Glaze, Nate & Santoya Dogan, Johnny & Kesha McKissick, Walter & Jackie Elliot, Marcus Linen, Marcus Fox, Tascha Byrd, L. Corrine Grant, Vivian Steadman, Corey Short, Toya James, Rashmi Khare, Ken & Angela Manigault, all the subscribers to the weekly "Faith Flow", every fan on my writer's page F.L.I.T.E., on Facebook, my friends in Cape Town, South Africa, everyone who has encouraged me through the years, and especially to you… the person reading this right now.

ABOUT THE AUTHOR

Rev. Demeterius "FLITE" Smith is a man of example who loves the Word of God and believes its careful use produces good fruit in the life of the believer. Born in the rural community of Dorchester, SC, Demeterius's early years were infused with the small town values of hard work, the importance of family and the necessity of keeping one's word.

Now, with over 10 years as a licensed and ordained minister, and five years in cyber ministry, Demeterius continues to help believers use their words as seed to produce a desirable life's harvest. In 2005, he founded "Flow With FLITE", a weekly online ministry where he uses his gift of poetry to creatively teach the word of God. That ministry continues today as "Faith Flow". Believers are regularly challenged to bring their thoughts and words in line with biblical truth.

Demeterius's first book, "Strength 2 Shine", was written in 2002 and is a compilation of his earlier poetic works. He is co-founder of Decree Publishing, which promises to be a full-service, Christ-centered publishing company. The Lovely Hill Baptist Association licensed Demeterius in 1998, and ordained him in 1999. In 2007, he received ordination from Redemption Ministerial Fellowship International, a global ministry of Redemption World Outreach Center in Greenville, SC.

Demeterius is an investor in the lives of youth. He recently ministered to children in Cape Town, South Africa, and volunteers with Operation GO!, inner city youth evangelism in Greenville. His unique delivery of the word of God helps youth understand its practical application in their daily lives and gives them a call to action in their daily lifestyle.

Demeterius has been given a gift of wisdom beyond his years. He uses that wisdom as consultant and coach to individuals and organizations.

Demeterius is a 2002 graduate of Clemson University, where he earned his degree in business management. He shares life with his wife, Deneshia, who also has a heart for ministry and knows the power of the spoken word. They make their home in Greenville, South Carolina.

Join FLITE's blog at www.flitesfaithflow.wordpress.com

For speaking engagements, contact info is as follows:

FLITE@lifedecreed.com / 864-735-3133

DECREE™
PUBLISHING

The ABC's of Taking Care of Your Pastor

WARNING: Common sense and common courtesy can change your pastor's life in extraordinary ways!

- Is your pastor overworked with increasing demands to meet?

- Would you like to learn how to show your pastor appreciation and consideration?

- Do you love your pastor?

- Are you concerned about your pastor's well being?

In *The ABC's of Taking Care of Your Pastor*, Demeterius "FLITE" Smith offers a powerful and practical guide that will teach congregations how to honor their pastor and his or her family in ways that are consistent and needed. Available Fall 2010.

Strength To Shine

Jesus Christ within is the strength everyone needs to truly shine!

Regardless of who you are, where you're from, past mistakes or current failures, God is willing and waiting to be glorified through your life. Dream your dreams, write the visions, use your talents — shine!

Strength To Shine is a reissue of Demeterius "FLITE" Smith's first book which was originally published in 2002. It contains FLITE's earlier poetry (written between 1994 and 2002) on love, friendship, faith, and life. Experience the writings of FLITE before *Faith Flow*. Available Summer 2010.

To receive product updates, news and events from Decree Publishing, join our e-mailing list! Send an email with your name to info@lifedecreed.com.

RECEIVING SALVATION

No matter who you are or what you have done, God is willing to forgive you.

In the beginning, God and Adam, the first man enjoyed a close relationship. But when Adam sinned and disobeyed God, the result was death. Not only would Adam and all mankind die physically, mankind became separated from God – a spiritual death. Man's close relationship with God was lost and every person thereafter would be born into sin. All mankind entered a "fallen" state of being. (See Genesis Chapters 1 – 3)

Mankind was instructed to offer animal sacrifices to make atonement for their sins. But this did not solve the dilemma of eternal separation from God. God does not want to be separated from us. So, God sent Jesus, His only begotten son to earth to become our lasting sacrifice and savior. Through a miraculous birth, Jesus was conceived by the Holy Spirit in a virgin named Mary. Because Jesus was born of a woman and of the Holy Spirit, he was fully God and fully man. Jesus lived without sin.

Because Jesus was without sin He was able to become the sacrifice that would make atonement for the sins of all of mankind. Jesus paid our sin debt in full. He did this by willingly dying on the cross for all of our sins (past, present and future). (See Matthew Chapters 1,2,27)

After three days God raised Jesus from the dead as the first born of many brethren. Jesus ascended into heaven and now sits at the right hand of God the Father where He intercedes on our behalf. When we accept Jesus Christ as our Lord and Savior, what we are saying is that we acknowledge that we are sinners and that we accept the payment that Jesus made on our behalf. (See Matthew Chapter 28)

When we accept what God sent Jesus to do for us this allows us to be reconnected (have our relationship restored) to God. By having our relationship restored with God through acceptance of Jesus Christ we access eternal life with God. If we don't accept what Jesus Christ did for us than that means our sin debt has not been satisfied. Those who will not accept Jesus as their savior will be held personally responsible for their sins – which is a price no man can pay.

Since Jesus was the only one capable of paying sins cost, those who do not accept Jesus Christ will remain separated from God for eternity. The good news for us is that God wants to have a personal relationship with us and that it doesn't matter what we have done. God knows all about you and He loves you so much that He used Jesus Christ as a way for you to be forgiven and reconnected to Him. (See Romans Chapter 10; 1 John Chapter 1)

DO YOU WANT TO GIVE YOUR LIFE TO GOD?

Romans 10:9-10 NKJV™ says:

"That if you confess with your mouth the Lord Jesus and believe in your heart that God has raised Him from the dead, you will be saved. For with the heart one believes unto righteousness, and with the mouth confession is made unto salvation."

This is a suggested prayer for salvation based on Romans 10:9

(Please pray out loud, whispering counts)

"Lord Jesus, I am a sinner and I stand in need. I come to you in prayer to ask for the salvation that you made available through your death on the cross. I believe God raised you from the dead and I confess that you are Lord. Please come into my heart and lead me forward in your will. It's in your name I pray, amen."

(If you invited Jesus Christ into your life today and have questions, please e-mail me, FLITE@lifedecreed.com, or speak with a pastor in your area).

www.ingramcontent.com/pod-product-compliance
Lightning Source LLC
Chambersburg PA
CBHW061319110426
42742CB00012BA/2252